W9-AGB-636

Crop Chemophobia

Crop Chemophobia

Will Precaution
Kill the Green Revolution?

Jon Entine, Editor

The AEI Press

Publisher for the American Enterprise Institute

WASHINGTON, D.C.

Distributed by arrangement with the Rowman & Littlefield Publishing Group, 4501 Forbes Boulevard, Suite 200, Lanham, Maryland 20706. To order, call toll free 1-800-462-6420 or 1-717-794-3800. For all other inquiries, please contact AEI Press, 1150 Seventeenth Street, N.W., Washington, D.C. 20036, or call 1-800-862-5801.

Library of Congress Cataloging-in-Publication Data

Crop chemophobia : will precaution kill the green revolution? /
Jon Entine, editor.
p. cm.
  Includes bibliographical references and index.
  ISBN-13: 978-0-8447-4361-5 (cloth)
  ISBN-10: 0-8447-4361-5 (cloth)
  ISBN-13: 978-0-8447-4363-9 (ebook)
  ISBN-10: 0-8447-4363-1 (ebook)
  1. Pesticides—Environmental aspects. 2. Environmental risk assessment.
I. Entine, Jon. II. American Enterprise Institute for Public Policy Research.
[DNLM: 1. Food Contamination—prevention & control—Europe. 2. Food
Contamination—prevention & control—United States. 3. Conservation of
Natural Resources—Europe. 4. Conservation of Natural Resources—United
States. 5. Food Supply—Europe. 6. Food Supply—United States. 7. Pesticides—
adverse effects—Europe. 8. Pesticides—adverse effects—United States.
9. Public Policy—Europe. 10. Public Policy—United States. WA 701]
  QH545.P4C76 2010
  363.17'92—dc22

Printed in the United States of America

Contents

List of Illustrations

Introduction:
Food, Pests, and the
Chemical Conundrum

Jon Entine

The plea to "save the earth" is resonant and critically important to a sustainable future. But what does that mean in practice? Every action indeed does lead to a reaction. This complex world is interlinked, and well-meaning initiatives are often twisted by unintended consequences. When it comes to public policy, prudence is important. Risks need to be examined in the light of not only rewards but also the likelihood of generating new, unforeseen risks. Sometimes the balance between saving the earth and saving humans can be lost. This is a book about understanding and preserving that balance.

If the loudest voices in the environmental movement are to be believed, we are on the edge of ecological Armageddon because of the threat of chemical contamination posed by modern agricultural farming. "Name a vegetable, and I'll tell you how dangerous it is," says Brian Hill, senior scientist for the Pesticide Action Network (PAN), the advocacy group leading the campaign to ban many agricultural chemicals. I name broccoli, my daughter's favorite vegetable. His voice turns grave. "The United States Department of Agriculture tested 671 samples in 2007," he says. "Forty different residues showed up. Five are known or possible carcinogens; nineteen are suspected hormone disrupters; three can cause developmental or reproductive problems; nine are considered neurotoxins."

According to Hill, 1,100 pesticides can be found in the U.S. food supply. In Europe, he claims, there are far fewer cases of pesticide residues: 350. And under European Union (EU) rules, only sixteen of the forty chemicals found on U.S. broccoli samples are approved for use. By his judgment, and that of many environmentalists with a visceral reaction against the word "chemical," that means the EU is safer and more responsible. Dad alert. Am I feeding my trusting preteen daughter lethal greens? PAN's statistics indeed sound frightening. But is her broccoli dangerous? Do "lax" U.S. regulations on pesticides pose a danger to American consumers? Would it be healthier for my family to pull up roots from Cincinnati, where we live, and resettle in Paris or Berlin?

Already more restrictive on regulating agricultural chemicals than the United States, the European Parliament in 2009 passed even more stringent standards. One of the most contentious issues for European farming in the past decade has been the interaction between methods of production and human health. The twenty-seven EU governments reached a consensus to institute criteria that could ultimately blacklist twenty-two chemicals—about 15 percent of the EU pesticide and herbicide market. Proponents of the new regulations hail them as precautions necessary to address the unknown cumulative effect of chemical residue.

The substances have been linked, in a scattering of laboratory studies on animals, to cancer, endangering reproduction or damaging genes. The ban, to be phased in beginning in 2011, has been challenged by some policy experts who believe the health risks are nonexistent, or vanishingly remote at worst, and are concerned that a ban could damage food security while yielding limited or no health benefits. Opponents also argue that the measures could lead to unforeseen consequences, such as damaging disease-control efforts in developing countries.

Is the EU being appropriately cautious? Or are government officials putting politics ahead of deliberative science? Are regulators, in imposing such sharp restrictions, responding to advances in risk monitoring, or are they reacting to a superfluous abundance of caution or even hysteria? This volume of essays attempts to address these questions. It emerged out of a 2009 conference on agricultural chemicals held at the American Enterprise Institute. The event brought together a broad collection of scientists, policymakers, media, and advocacy group activists from across the ideological spectrum. All were asked to provide essays for this book, and many did.

Toxic Limits

In order to maintain healthy crops, farmers fight a constant battle against insects, fungi, and plant diseases, as well as weeds that compete with the crops for water, nutrients, and light, all of which make harvesting more difficult. Advanced modern agricultural chemical technology has helped prevent infectious diseases and enhanced crop yields. Pesticides and herbicides protect crops against weeds, insects, and fungus. They are one of the drivers of the Green Revolution, which has dramatically cut world hunger in the past sixty years. Agricultural chemicals are also among the most scrutinized and regulated of all technologies. The undeniable reality is that none of us wants toxins as a side dish. So we as a society need to make sure that what we consume is safe. That's where this issue gets thorny—and political.

The heart of the controversy is the debate over risk versus hazard. Risk describes the probability that dangers are documentable. The key is setting the threshold. Under the hammer of government regulators, scientists are ultra-cautious—setting distant limits below levels at which tests on laboratory animals show that a substance is likely to accumulate in the human body and even hint at potential dangers. Following long-standing worldwide scientific protocol, chemicals are considered safe if, on the basis of established studies on animals, they pose no known risk to our health at a thousand or more times the level found in food. So long as a substance is found below that thousandfold threshold, it has been allowed onto the market. But with advances in chemical testing equipment, scientists are able to measure chemicals in parts per billion and even parts per trillion, putting pressure to raise thresholds even higher—even absent evidence that the current standards are in any way inadequate.

The standards for approving chemicals trace back to 1959, when the United States faced a cancer panic linked to food. Microscopic traces of a synthetic herbicide that was a carcinogen in rodents were detected in cranberries. It was pointed out at the time that one would need to eat fifteen thousand pounds of cranberries every day of one's life to match the dose rodents were given, but that sense of proportion was lost in the hysteria. There have been many food chemical scares since then: DDT, dioxin, nitrites in bacon and sausage, alar in apples. Cancer is admittedly scary, and for years very little was known about the biochemical mechanisms involved in cancer etiology, and even less about how our immune system defends us against it. But now we know much more and have developed a variety of tests to evaluate the carcinogenicity of chemicals and their role in affecting the flow of our hormones. But what do those tests really reveal when it comes to human health and safety?

In fact, most of us have more to fear from natural chemicals than artificial ones. The notion that because a substance is "natural" it is somehow safer than one that is artificial or synthetic is spurious. The perception that pesticides are dangerous because they are "chemicals" is embedded in our society's collective consciousness. But look around—the plant kingdom harbors vast storehouses of "natural" chemicals that are far more dangerous than anything chemists could ever hope to synthesize in their labs. And these phytochemicals are affecting us at a far greater rate than are the bioaccumulated synthetic ones. Plants have had millions of years to evolve an arsenal of nasty natural pesticides to safeguard them from their enemies.

The renowned molecular biologist and biochemist Bruce Ames, for whom the Ames test is named, estimates that 99.99 percent of all pesticides (by weight) are natural; thus, we are ingesting about ten thousand times more natural than synthetic pesticides. Virtually all the carcinogens in our environment are natural, and many, if not all, of the foods we eat contain thousands of different chemicals, only some of which are rodent carcinogens. Apples, bananas, basil, cabbage, citrus fruits, mushrooms, turnips, and many more foods contain naturally occurring chemicals that are toxic—they cause cancer at large lifelong doses in laboratory rodents.

So, how dangerous is that conventionally grown broccoli? Despite the hysteria generated by PAN, which is campaigning to ban or restrict many chemicals long deemed safe, broccoli is known to be protective against cancer in humans when eaten at realistic levels over a lifetime, probably because it contains high levels of various natural antioxidants. Studies of conventionally grown agriculture indicate that 65 percent of all samples show no chemical residue. Microscopic amounts of at least four different possible human carcinogens (based on rodent testing) are indeed common.

Those with minute chemical residues could be easily washed. The tiny amount that might be consumed falls well below established minimum safety levels. Now, if you ate ten or twenty pounds of broccoli every day of your life, you just might increase by a tiny fraction of a percent your risk of some cancer or other.

Questions of dose and risk are at the heart of the controversy over whether a chemical should be considered dangerous or not. It might be helpful to review just how chemicals are tested and restrictions are generated:

(1) Scientists do a biological assay known as an Ames test on some pesticide, food additive, preservative, or whatever to find out if it is mutagenic. It tests whether the bacteria's DNA is altered in a significant way.

(2) If the chemical is confirmed as mutagenic, studies are then undertaken to determine what is called the "maximum tolerated dose" of this chemical in rats or mice. The maximum tolerated dose is the amount of the chemical that almost kills a rodent in a single dose. It is also a dose that, depending on the particular chemical, can be thousands to millions of times higher than a human could ever eat in a lifetime.

(3) Next, the rodents are fed just 10 percent less than the maximum tolerated dose daily for their entire one- to two-year lifetime. However, many chemicals cannot be fed to rodents because the substances are so noxious at the dosages given. So scientists skip trying to mimic how humans are exposed to the chemical and just take the easy route and use gavage (that is, inject the chemical into the animal's gut every day).

(4) After a year or two, the rodents are killed, and scientists count up all the tumors the animals might have accumulated in various organs. Most of the rodents in the control group, fed a normal diet, will have various tumors anyway because they have been bred to be cancer prone.

So, if the test group of rodents fed—or more likely injected with—some noxious chemical at the highest dose has an average of, say, four tumors per animal in a particular organ, and the control group has an average of only one tumor per animal, then the chemical being tested is said to increase cancer incidence by 400 percent. Does this mean that such a study proves a chemical will cause adverse effects in rats, let alone humans? No. Does it mean that this preliminary finding will end up in a headline or in a media release from one group or another attempting to use preliminary research to support a cause or movement? Anyone with access to the Internet knows the answer to that question.

(5) Next, under pressure from the suddenly energized media and advocacy groups, a political body, such as the European Parliament or the U.S. Congress, or a regulatory body, such as the Food and Drug Administration, will classify this chemical as a possible human carcinogen, as if rodents were nothing more than miniature humans, and establish acceptable levels of the chemical in foods—using a huge margin-of-safety factor based on mathematical models that no one, chemophobes or industry apologists, believes is meaningful.

Yet that's the very model that led the EU to issue its latest restrictions on agricultural chemicals. Under the circumstances, it is not surprising that we have a full-blown crisis about how we understand, communicate about, and regulate chemicals.

Precautionary Politics

Although the environmental movement was birthed in the United States in the 1960s and 1970s, Europe now takes a more stringent approach to environmental regulation. New regulations are based on the "precautionary principle"—the notion that many chemicals are considered intrinsically dangerous at any level even absent definitive risk data. Growing out of the environmental and Green movements in Sweden and Germany, the precautionary principle has largely become the operative regulatory stand-ard in Europe. While it can be applied in areas as different as climate change and antitrust policy, one of the primary focuses of its advocates from the beginning has been the regulation of food and the modern technologies used to produce it.

The precautionary principle is difficult to define. It is more an attitude, or approach, than the kind of clear-cut rule that we generally think of as being the basis for law and regulation. Briefly defined, it posits that if any human activity raises a perceived threat of harm, immediate regulatory and legal sanctions should be imposed even if no cause-and-effect relationship can be established scientifically. It is a regulatory standard, not a science standard. As such it gives legislators and regulators the freedom to pick and choose which substances to restrict or ban. Simply the perception of the possibility of a problem is enough to justify its invocation. In its most extreme application, no trade-offs can be considered, such as the harm that might be caused from the ban on a particular activity or technology; no consideration is given as to whether the potential economic costs of regu-lation outweigh the potential benefits. It's what's called a hazard standard, and it has slowly come to replace the risk standard long used in the United States and in most of the rest of the world.

Various shades of the precautionary principle have been integrated into the EU's regulatory system over the past fifteen years. It has also been at work in justifying Europe's move away from risk-based calculations in all areas of science. It has been the basis for that continent's ongoing ban on genetically modified (GM) foods and GM agricultural crops, despite the fact that there have never been any documented health consequences associated with the biotechnology. It has also been invoked to justify Europe's wide-spread bans on agricultural chemicals, which have been put in place with-out regard to and often in direct contradiction to the advice of European scientists and safety and health authorities. The new ban was passed into law with no assessment of the impacts on the farming industry.

Environmental activists do claim support among some scientists. Professor Vyvyan Howard, toxicopathologist at the University of Ulster, and a member of the UK Advisory Committee on Pesticides, says, "It has been my position for many years that a precautionary reduction in the levels of the most hazardous pesticides by substitution makes good sense.

The fetus and infant are particularly vulnerable to exposure. The EU proposal to use hazard assessment is a pragmatic way forward."[1]

But most scientists, even those who actively research alternatives to traditional pesticides, have reacted warily at best to the blacklist. As a rule, they believe they are not pro-chemical but pro-crop-protection, which has international food security as its central focus. All food production carries some degree of risk. They ask, "What risks are acceptable, and how do you manage them?" Rather than focusing myopically on relatively affluent European consumers, they take a broader perspective, looking at the risk to financially squeezed European farmers, whose crop output and income will be cut, and to developing countries, which will have to pay higher prices for European agricultural exports.

The UK Pesticides Safety Directorate claims that the blacklist will damage farming and provide few health benefits. "There was potential for up to 100 percent yield loss on carrots," it warns. Onions and parsnips would also be seriously affected, with a 20 percent fall in crop yields for cereals. The EU ban will have "genuinely alarming consequences," says Ian Denholm, head of the Plant and Invertebrate Ecology Department at Rothamsted Research Institute in Hertfordshire, United Kingdom, the oldest and most renowned independent agricultural research center in the world. Denholm and some 160 other leading scientists throughout the world signed a petition opposing the regulations, contending that traditional science was being abandoned under pressure from politicians responding to hysterical constituents. The new rules, they say, show "a worrying lack of concern for the real risks to health and development to which most people in developing countries are exposed."[2]

Agricultural scientists take seriously their responsibility to balance competing risks—the potential dangers to the environment or human health from using a particular chemical versus the economic and health benefits that increased food yields, particularly in the developing world, will yield. Crops account for more than 40 percent of world exports in primary products, with Europe trailing only the United States as provider to the world's food basket. Europe produces about 16 percent of the developing world's cereal grains and substantial amounts of its fruits and vegetables. The blacklist will cut production at a time when policy experts are warning that Europe must double its output by 2050 to deal with the effects of population growth and climate change. A report issued in April 2010 by the Group of Eight nations warns that the food crisis of the past two years "will become structural in only a few decades" unless production is dramatically ramped up.

The new rules are changing the way in which pesticides are being regulated, moving from risk-based assessments (based on the real-world application of pesticides) to hazard-based assessments (based strictly on laboratory data). Do we really want to be telling the hungry of the world to persist on a diet of precaution? "As a region favorable for crop production, Europe cannot opt out of its responsibility to be part of the world," says John Lucas, Denholm's colleague at Rothamsted. "We may not have to worry here because no one goes hungry and we can afford higher prices. But that's not true elsewhere. This is about food security. We have a moral responsibility to feed the hungry." He is exasperated by the new restrictions. "I have kids," he says. "I obviously don't want them to eat toxin-laced food. But the critics are driven by emotion. We have to be sensible about this and also responsible to everyone and not just focus on our fears."[3]

"Unfortunately, the EU's agricultural and pest management policies are currently heading in the opposite direction, actively reducing the options available to farmers without adequate scientific assessment of risk," says Friedhelm Schmider, director-general of the Brussels-based European Crop Protection Association.[4] Another big fear, say scientists, is that the restrictions could backfire and create a new generation of more dangerous fungal crops, weeds, and insects that quickly become resistant to a more limited palette of chemicals

Despite massive evidence of the relative safety of most agricultural chemicals, there are regular campaigns against specific or even all pesticides, very often orchestrated by the same nongovernmental organizations (NGOs) that appear to have opposition to technology at the heart of their raison d'être. These groups are often very good at what they do. They are well connected, they use media communications well, and they are expert at creating political pressure on regulatory agencies. The science is often not supportive of their positions. This is why the precautionary principle is so important to them. It is vague enough, they recognize, that if they can create enough political pressure, it can be invoked to restrict, suspend, or ban a chemical, whatever the balance of evidence says. The legal and regulatory consequence in Europe, and increasingly in the United States, is a succession of highly charged, highly politicized battles over many key technologies, not just in agriculture.

This new EU decision breaks with long-standing protocol in the United States and many other countries that rely primarily on risk standards, which hold that chemicals are considered safe if studies on animals reveal no known risks at the levels found in food, with huge margins of risk built in. Some people propose replacing this well-developed risk assessment framework with the vagaries and uncertainty that would result from a highly politicized precautionary approach. That would be bad for farmers, as critical tools for productivity would be lost, and bad for consumers, as food prices rise. It would be bad for future innovation in new technologies, because the risks of making a development decision will be increased. It would certainly be bad for productivity at a time when food security is a critical topic at the top of government agendas worldwide, and bad for the economy as a whole.

The Chapters

Does the EU's new approach to pesticides place the scientific method in jeopardy? What are the implications of the precautionary standard, which may shape future regulations in many other countries? How is the tension between public advocacy groups and regulators affecting policy decisions on agricultural chemicals?

The first two chapters in this book lay out the dimensions of the current controversy. In chapter 1, Euros Jones, director of regulatory affairs at the European Crop Protection Association, outlines the regulatory landscape for agricultural chemicals in Europe and hints at problems to come in other countries. Chapter 2, by Jonathan Adler, director of the Center for Business Law and Regulation at the Case Western Reserve University School of Law, reviews the legal history of the precautionary principle, which is at the center of the regulatory debate over chemicals.

The middle section of the book presents three intriguing case studies. In chapter 3, I present the story of atrazine, whose benefits and comparatively benign risk profile have made it one of the world's most popular agricultural chemicals, but also the central target of many NGOs. In chapter 4, Mark Whalon, an entomologist who directs the Pesticide Alternatives Laboratory at Michigan State University, and his colleague, Jeanette Wilson, deconstruct the rocky regulatory road of one crop, the tart cherry, and how the push for alternative pesticides impacts public perceptions and regulations. In Chapter 5, Richard Tren, director of Africa Fighting Malaria, goes behind the headlines to help us understand the half-century debate over DDT and its consequences for environmental and human health.

Finally we wrap up the book with two essays reviewing policy implications. Claude Barfield, a resident scholar at the American Enterprise Institute, discusses in chapter 6 the debate over pesticides from the perspective of the World Trade Organization, which demands that regulatory decisions affecting trade be based on proof of harm and not just speculative fear—in other words, on empirical science. Finally, in chapter 7, Doug Nelson of CropLife America and his colleague Alexander Rinkus outline the challenges of feeding a still-booming world population.

Notes

1. "Plans to Ban Dozens of Pesticides will 'Lead to Food Shortages and Send Prices Rising Further,'" *Daily Mail*, July 2, 2008, http://www.dailymail.co.uk/news/article-1031265/Plans-ban-dozens-pesticides-lead-food-shortages-send-prices-rising-further.html.

2. Sharon Davis, "EU Pesticide Ban 'Will Harm Malaria Control,'" Science and Development Network, March 25, 2009, http://www.scidev.net/En/climate-change-and-energy/health-policy/news/eu-pesticide-ban-will-harm-malaria-control-.html.

3. Interview with author, May 25, 2009.

4. "G8 Warns World Needs to Double Food Output by 2050," European Crop Protection Association, April 8, 2009, http://www.ecpa.be/en/newsroom/press-releases/_doc/18592/.

PART I

Perspective

1

European Pesticides and Herbicides in the Crosshairs

Euros Jones

The consensus reached by twenty-seven European Union governments to institute new criteria could ultimately blacklist a significant number of important chemicals used by the agricultural and pest control industries. The most controversial aspect of the new regulation is the rejection of the traditional scientific use of "risk analysis," which measures the potential impact of substances on humans, with a more restrictive "hazard" structure, which contends that some chemicals are intrinsically dangerous at any level, even absent evidence of definitive risk. The formulation of the new regulation raises provocative questions about the legislative process and the future role of science in shaping policy decisions, as well as wider political issues. The new legislation also has been challenged by some policy experts concerned that it could damage food security while yielding limited or no health benefits.

How Did the Legislative Process Evolve?

The text for the new regulation replaces legislation that has been in place since 1991—Directive 91/414/EEC. The review program accompanying this directive led to the removal of many pesticide-active substances from the EU market. Approximately 350 chemicals now remain approved for use, compared with nearly 1,000 substances that were available at the start of the program.

The process to amend the EU legislation started in July 2001 with the publication by the European Commission of a ten-year progress report.[1] This report highlighted many of the key developments under the 1991 directive and identified a number of areas that would require further consideration.

Following the publication of the commission's report, the Council of Ministers and the European Parliament were given the opportunity to comment.[2] Both bodies provided remarks on the need to introduce criteria for the approval of active substances, with the European Parliament in particular requesting the *"exclusion of substances with a very hazardous profile."* Although this view was accepted by the parliament, most stakeholders believed at the time that such a provision was unlikely to be included in any legislative proposal.

The European Commission was expected to come forward in 2002 with a proposal to amend the directive. This action was delayed, however, largely because regulatory authorities were focused on reviewing all the agricultural chemicals on the EU market at that time. Little progress was made in the development of the proposal until 2005, when a draft proposal was circulated for discussion to stakeholders and the member states. This proposal raised a number of concerns, and the commission agreed that an impact assessment would need to be carried out in order to better understand the potential impact of the new elements being proposed for inclusion in an amended legislative framework.

We should note that at this stage the European Commission's draft proposal did not include hazard-based cutoff criteria, and the impact assessment that was planned at that stage did not consider the impact of introducing such criteria. Only after the completion of the impact assessment in early 2006 did the proposal for a new regulation evolve to include the hazard-based cutoff criteria. The introduction of these criteria followed a difficult decision-making procedure for a number of active substances that were under consideration for listing on Annex I of Directive 91/414/EEC—the EU's approved list of active substances. Having recognized the difficult political implications related to these substances, the College of Commissioners decided to include certain hazard-based cutoff criteria, as they believed this would smooth the process ahead.[3]

The European Commission's proposal for a regulation to replace Directive 91/414/EEC was eventually published in July 2006, paving the way for a negotiation under the co-decision procedure, whereby in most cases two or more readings by the Council of Ministers and the parliament are required before a final decision is taken. The first reading of the European Parliament was completed in September 2007, with the "Common position" of the Council of Ministers completed twelve months later.[4]

What Changes Were Proposed in the Negotiations?

While the commission proposal included a number of hazard-based cutoff criteria, the first reading of the European Parliament proposed numerous additional criteria. The Environment Committee of the European Parliament, the lead committee on this dossier, largely drove these additional criteria. These criteria included bee toxicity, neurotoxicity, and immunotoxicity, as well as more restrictive interpretations of the other criteria put forward in the commission's initial proposal. These additional criteria were put forward in close collaboration with a number of the NGOs that were heavily involved in the dossier, and largely focused on issues that were being discussed in the European media at the time (in particular the loss of bee colonies, where a link was being made to pesticides), as well as other policy areas in which NGOs were active at that time.

In putting forward these criteria, the parliament was unaware of the potential agricultural impact. Only after these changes were proposed did it become clear that these additional criteria could (in a worst-case scenario) lead to the loss of nearly 80 percent of the active substances on the market at that time. Although a number of the members of the European Parliament leading the discussion challenged these figures, it was generally accepted within the parliament that their first reading would lead to an unacceptable situation, one that would severely hinder EU agricultural production. The second reading of the parliament was carried out against this backdrop, and this led to the consideration of a less radical solution. The final text, although it introduced a number of changes, was similar to the commission's initial proposal, which included a number of provisions that strengthened certain criteria while also ensuring flexibility in maintaining solutions where a clear agricultural need existed.

The Hazard-Based Cutoff (Rejection) Criteria

Various cutoff criteria are included in the final regulation. These criteria include:

- **Persistent Organic Pollutants**—POPs are defined under the Stockholm Convention and are usually considered as substances that trigger four separate criteria: persistence, bio-accumulation, toxicity, and long-range transport.

- **PBT**—This is the EU criterion for **P**ersistence, **B**io-accumulation, and **T**oxicity. Although the three criteria in PBT are also mentioned in the POPs criteria, we should note that the values used to trigger the criteria are substantially different.

- **vPvB**—This is another EU-based criterion for **v**ery **P**ersistent and **v**ery **B**io-accumulative.

- **CMR category 1 and 2**—These are substances that are "known or presumed to have the potential" to cause such effects as **C**arcinogens or **M**utagens or as being toxic to **R**eproduction. This criterion applies to substances that are currently or are to be classified under the given categories.

- **Endocrine disrupters**—Although definitions have been developed for endocrine-disrupting chemicals, no sound scientific criteria have yet been developed to identify those substances that will be classed as "endocrine disrupters."

"Endocrine Disruption"

Endocrine disruption has been a major factor in the discussion over the entire period of the negotiations because, as noted above, there is currently no clarity regarding the criteria in place. Although a high-level definition has been agreed on, little work has been done to set out detailed scientific criteria in practice, and thus that remains a major focus for the European Commission.[5] Such a scientific definition is required not only for the pesticide legislation but also for REACH (Registration,

Evaluation, and Authorisation of Chemicals), the EU's general legislative framework for chemicals.

The uncertainty regarding the criteria for endocrine disruption has also led to much discussion about the impact of the cutoff criteria. As a worst case, some analysts have suggested that more than thirty substances could be impacted by a very restrictive definition of endocrine disruption. However, the expectation of most policymakers is that the figure will be lower. But this will only become clear once the criteria are in place and the substances have been evaluated against those criteria, which could take a number of years.

Which Substances Will Be Affected by the Cutoff Criteria?

There have been numerous claims about the number of active substances that will be affected by the newly adopted cutoff criteria. The European Parliament claimed in January 2009 that the new criteria would lead to the removal of twenty-two active substances that were identified. However, we should note that these substances were identified as potentially being affected and that no final decision has been taken on their fate or on that of any other substances. We should also remember that these substances have already passed a strict EU risk evaluation and are currently being used by farmers to protect a wide range of crops. Indeed, in some cases, the European Commission has recently decided to approve the active substances in question for a period of ten years.

Note also that the impact of the cutoff criteria would not be immediate. The fate of each chemical will be assessed at the scheduled date of reevaluation and reapproval. All active substances currently on the EU market will go through a reapproval process. This process has already started, but most substances are to be evaluated between 2014 and 2019.

Cutoffs and the Derogation Clause

Although the cutoff criteria have been included in the final legislation, there has been some recognition that the criteria could lead to the removal of active chemicals that play an important part in crop protection. The new regulation therefore includes a derogation clause to maintain a product on the market where it is "necessary to control a serious danger to plant health." The introduction of this clause raises a number of important points, in particular:

- It recognizes that the hazard-based criteria do not rest solely on safety concerns but rather on political considerations. Although many supporters of the cutoff criteria have claimed that the measures are based on safety and the need to give further guarantees, the fact that the criteria can be bypassed underlines the fact that these substances can continue to be used safely for crop protection.

- As the clause is restrictive, it will discourage industry from investing in any substances that meet the criteria. It will, however, ensure the maintenance of solutions of major importance for European farmers. Many of the identified chemicals play important parts in crop protection management strategies, and, if it is applied, this derogation will help reduce the risk of further resistance to the remaining crop protection solutions, therefore ensuring that agricultural production is more sustainable.

Food Safety in a European Context

The new regulation, and the process by which it was reached, raises many questions. Clearly, it should not be considered in isolation: it is necessary to look beyond the world of plant protection and consider the regulation's relationship to other policy areas and to the broader political issues.

The process followed for reaching agreement on the new regulation raises a number of questions about the role of sound scientific advice in the decision-making process in the European Union. At the outset, the European Commission assumed that such criteria would "increase the level of protection given to human health…and the environment, through a series of new provisions….The safety evaluations of active substances will be founded on strict criteria, also based on health considerations and the effects on the environment (e.g., persistence in the environment)."[6]

Although the commission claimed that the hazard criteria would improve both health and environmental protection, this was not supported by any independent scientific advice. In such a situation, where major new legislation is being proposed, it was unfortunate that independent scientific advice was never requested. There is still no inclination to request such advice before considering proposals with such serious potential impact.

Indeed, many experts in this area were readily available to the European Commission if it had sought such expertise. The European Food Safety Authority (EFSA) was set up in 2002 in part to "provide scientific advice and scientific and technical support for the Community's legislation…which have a direct or indirect impact on food and feed safety."[7] Questions must therefore be asked why the commission did not request such advice when a European authority had been specifically set up to provide it. It is not unreasonable to conclude that the proposal was drawn up based more on the perceptions of pesticides' impact rather than on objective and independent scientific evidence.

One of the most unsettling elements of EU policymaking on food safety issues generally is that policymakers are downplaying or ignoring sound scientific advice. Instead, political decisions are being made and then presented as measures intended to protect the consumer. This politicization is especially apparent in cases involving the EFSA, which was specifically set up to provide independent scientific advice on food issues. But member states of the European Union have often questioned the independent advice provided by the central agency and have refused to accept its guidance, challenging its advice as "too European" when they wanted to take more restrictive measures that reflected more parochial interests than those being considered at the European level.

This is especially true in the area of genetically modified organisms. The EFSA's advice about the safety of genetically modified organisms has been largely positive,[8] but no authorizations have been granted under the European decision-making process since the EFSA was set up. The reason for this blockage is that the majority of member states must support and vote in favor of the proposals being made, but an adequate majority has not been found for any proposal yet made. Rejecting the pan-European recommendations, some member states, such as Austria, Greece, and, more recently, Germany, have put additional restrictions in place that further limit the potential entry of genetically modified products.

Science and Political Contradictions

The handling of other controversial substances, such as chemicals used in the cosmetics industry, highlights the arbitrariness and political nature of the decision-making process. During the negotiations to amend the pesticide legislation, a parallel discussion was taking place on the possible amendment of the EU legislative framework for cosmetics. The use of hazard-based cutoff criteria was also a key issue in those discussions, but the conclusions reached were quite different.

In the pesticides arena, commissioners recommended that substances with a hazard classification as CMR category 1 and 2 (see details under point 4 on page 18) should be removed from the market. However, in the cosmetics discussions, commissioners made a clear move to ensure that such substances would be allowed to remain on the market. The arguments presented by the European Commission to defend the actions in both policy areas are particularly interesting and do highlight a lack of consistency. In the pesticide area, the responsible commissioner states that "it is obvious that removing some active substances with such extremely hazardous properties…would not have a detrimental effect on human health or the environment."[9] The statement made to support the commission's view on cosmetics states something very different, however: "The automatic ban without possibility of an exception for CMR 1 and 2 substances…without considering exposure and actual use of the substance…could lead to absurd situations.[10]

Why is there such a clear inconsistency in European policymaking? The answer to the question lies in the EU's conservative approach to food safety policymaking as opposed to other policy areas. This is partly linked to the hysteria generated by past food crises in Europe. It is also linked to the influence of activists, who are much more involved in food issues than in other policy areas such as cosmetics.

This lack of consistency is a source of concern for a number of industry stakeholders and also now appears to be a concern for the newly reappointed president of the commission, Manuel Barroso. Soon after his reappointment, Commissioner Barroso stressed his support for independent scientific review, stating, "In the next Commission, I want to set up a chief scientific adviser who has the power to deliver proactive, scientific advice throughout all stages of policy development and delivery."[11]

This appears to be a positive step, but we will need to wait and see whether an adviser, if appointed, will be given adequate freedom and independence to make a difference. Looking specifically at food safety issues, one could argue that a scientific adviser is already in place in the form of the European Food Safety Authority, and that what really needs to change is the commission's willingness to request advice—and then to follow it.

EU Leading the World in Food Safety?

The European Commission argues that its aim is to deliver the safest food for the European consumer—safer than anywhere else in the world. But is this really what the EU is doing? While much focus has been put on food safety in the European Union since the bovine spongiform encephalopathy (BSE) crisis, or "Mad Cow Disease," in the mid-1990s, many policies have been based on political perceptions and not on scientific advice. This is clearly the case both for plant protection products and for genetically modified organisms.

Because the EU is such a large trading bloc, it influences legislative developments in other countries. The policies of the EU are often copied in other markets and especially in those countries where the EU is an important export market for agricultural products. Although many of the measures in the EU do improve overall food safety, their policies for plant protection products and genetically modified organisms (GMOs) have the potential to have more negative influences that impact the agricultural productivity of other countries without any food safety benefits.

Given the impact on these countries, the EU does have a responsibility to ensure that its legislation takes into account the impact on producers and markets outside the EU. This can best be done by ensuring that the best scientific advice is being followed—and by promoting change in countries based on that scientific advice and not being based on perceptions that are increasingly seen as political drivers, particularly in more affluent states such as those in the EU.

The Influence of NGOs

Nongovernmental organizations clearly play an important role in influencing policymakers in the EU and worldwide. NGOs appear to be particularly influential in European decision making on food safety issues. Looking at the decision-making process for the pesticide legislation, we can see that the most active NGOs were those opposed to pesticide use (such as the Pesticide Action Network) and environmental NGOs, such as Friends of the Earth and Greenpeace.

Intriguingly, most of the arguments of the "environmental" NGOs focused on consumer protection and not environmental protection. In fact, they appeared to make a concerted effort to stay away from discussions about the environment. From one perspective, it is difficult to understand why the consumer protection NGOs kept out of this debate, as consumer and environmental protection are both equally important in pesticide policymaking. However, the relative power and influence of the NGOs would appear to be an important influencing factor—with the consumer protection NGOs more poorly equipped to put forward their views when having to "compete" with the resources and media reach available to the environmental NGOs. As a consequence, the views and needs of the general consumer are not put forward as aggressively, and often they are lost in the political debate.

Although many of the NGOs complain that the chemical industry unduly influences political decision makers, this does not accord with the facts. In the European Parliament especially, the NGOs have a strong presence and a strong influence over the advisers (or "assistants," as they are called in Brussels) to the members of the European Parliament. Because these political advisers often have limited professional experience and usually have little or no expert scientific advice available to them, many of their decisions can be influenced by the simple and populist messages of NGOs.

In addition, the NGOs are often well represented in the European Parliament because many parliament staffers have previously worked for NGOs. This was especially the case in the discussions on the pesticide legislation, where the key adviser to the lead member of the European Parliament had worked for various NGOs and could not be portrayed as representing a balanced view of the whole parliament.

The Precautionary Principle

The precautionary principle is often cited in the EU as a reason for adopting certain policy measures, and this has especially been the case in the food safety arena. The commission itself maintains that "the precautionary principle…should in particular be taken into consideration in the fields of environmental protection and human, animal and plant health."[12]

The commission's communication on the precautionary principle is a rational and admirable policy document that highlights the importance of the scientific method, with the precautionary approach being taken when there is significant uncertainty. It is worth highlighting certain passages of the commission's document, including:

- Recourse to the precautionary principle presupposes a scientific evaluation of the risk, which because of the insufficiency of the data, their inconclusive or imprecise nature, makes it impossible to determine with sufficient certainty the risk in question.

- The implementation of an approach based on the precautionary principle should start with a scientific evaluation, as complete as possible, and where possible, identifying at each stage the degree of scientific uncertainty.

- Measures should be consistent with the measures already adopted in similar circumstances or using similar approaches.

In looking at the commission's own communication, it is hard to argue that this is an unacceptable and unscientific approach; it continuously advocates the consideration of new scientific evidence when it becomes available. The use of the precautionary principle is, however, often cited as a reason for taking political measures—where the decision on whether or not there is uncertainty takes place at a political and not at a scientific level. The commission's paper on the precautionary principle tries very hard to work within scientific parameters. Unfortunately, those scientific parameters are often ignored when decisions have to be made in certain policy areas.

The Precautionary Principle and the Hazard Criteria

As stated above, the precautionary principle has been invoked as one of the key arguments for taking certain food safety measures in the EU. It has been widely assumed that the hazard-based cutoff criteria have been put in place as a precautionary measure. The discussions in the European Parliament referred to the precautionary principle numerous times, and these references highlighted a willingness to use the precautionary principle as a means of justifying measures that are political and populist, rather than scientifically justifiable.

We should note, however, that the commission *has not* suggested that the use of hazard criteria was based on the precautionary principle. Rather, it has argued that it has concerns about the use of certain hazardous substances that it believes should be taken off the market. Although the precautionary principle has often been cited for taking measures that are more populist than precautionary, in this case, this has largely not been true.

The Impact on Agriculture and Food

The discussions on the new regulation took place as food prices peaked in Europe and worldwide. And although certain parties to the decision-making process maintained a very "green" agenda, there was a realization that plant protection products play a very important role in protecting our food and ensuring that adequate quantities of food are produced for a growing global population.

It is unfortunate that those pushing the "green" agenda believe that food can be produced without the use of plant protection products that have been used for many years and demonstrated through rigorous scientific testing to be safe when used appropriately. But the recent price spikes have shown the need to make the best use of the available resources. Of course, more land can be brought into production to ensure adequate food for a growing population, but this will clearly have a negative effect on the protection of biodiversity in more sensitive areas.

Making the best use of the available resources must include a policy to produce intensively on the best lands available, while at the same time ensuring that those lands remain productive for future generations. In addition to increasing productivity, today's agricultural technologies can also ensure that the use of the best land can be both intensive *and* sustainable.

While some of the tools available to support productive agriculture are being removed, we should note with concern that the increases in yields have slowed considerably over the last fifty years. While global yield increases averaged nearly 4 percent per annum over the period 1961–1990, the projection for the period 2000–2030 is a little over 1 percent.

Clearly, the removal of valuable tools under the new EU pesticide policy will lead to a further decline. Some projections of the impact of the new regulation suggest a yield impact of more than 20 percent if certain fungicides are taken off the EU market. Although at present we do not know how many of those substances may be removed, any reductions would have a major impact on EU agricultural production and the competitiveness of European farmers.

This point was made by the United Kingdom in the final stage of the negotiations on the new regulation. Negotiators highlighted in particular their concern on endocrine disrupting, stating that "no proper assessment of its potential impact on agriculture in the European Union, or of its benefits for consumers, is possible. The UK has repeatedly stressed the importance of understanding the impact of these measures before it could commit itself to the Regulation. Without this understanding, the EU risks taking measures which would have significant adverse impacts on crop protection but secure no significant health benefits for consumers."[13]

It is particularly important to note that the EU is taking this action at a time when the Food and Agriculture Organization is calling for a 70 percent increase in food production by 2050 to feed a growing world population.[14] There is an evident disconnect between policymaking on this issue and the wider issues linked to food production policy.

The Impact on Research and Innovation

During the discussion of the new regulation, it has often been suggested that it would boost innovation and offer new market opportunities. We should remember that certain elements of the new regulation are positive and offer new opportunities for industry to innovate and develop new markets. Over the last fifteen years, there has been a major consolidation of the innovative crop protection industry. In Europe alone, whereas there were eight companies researching and developing new chemistry in 1994, today there are only three. Although there are numerous reasons for this consolidation, one major driver was the need to remain competitive in the development of new chemistry. With escalating costs and tougher regulatory processes, synergies needed to be found, and this led to a large number of mergers and acquisitions in the late 1990s and into the 2000s. Today, it is widely agreed that there are only five companies that invest in the research and development of new chemistry, and further consolidation in the coming years is highly likely.

While the number of research-and-development-based companies has declined, the number of substances being screened has increased substantially. On average, 140,000 chemical substances are screened in order to find one new chemical that can be used in plant protection. With the introduction of the cutoff criteria, the hurdles for success have been raised, and the number of new solutions will likely decrease.

Looking specifically at the hazard-based cutoff criteria, some analysts have suggested that clear hazard criteria will provide more certainty for industry when deciding on its research priorities and would be a clear and early signal for industry to look for substances that do not meet these criteria. At first glance, this is a logical conclusion, but major uncertainty still exists regarding which substances will be categorized as meeting these cutoff criteria.

In making a decision on whether a substance actually triggers these criteria, experts will still need to carry out a detailed evaluation of all available data. Furthermore, it is often not a clear-cut decision if a substance actually triggers the criteria, and any decision will be highly influenced by the subjective interpretation of the evaluating experts. Although the investing company may believe that its substance does not trigger the criteria, there is an element of uncertainty, and no company will be willing to invest in a chemical even if there is a relatively low likelihood that the chemical would eventually be categorized unfavorably. At present, it costs more than two hundred million dollars to develop a new active substance, with around one hundred million dollars of that cost being spent on the development of safety data for the chemical. A company is therefore unlikely to spend that amount of money when there is a 25 percent risk that the product will not be allowed to enter such a key market as the European Union.

Basing decisions on one criterion alone will also lead to a situation where a new substance will not be brought to market (or will not be allowed to enter the market) even though its overall safety profile is extremely favorable compared to the products currently on the market. For example, a substance that poses a very low level of risk to humans and the environment following a detailed risk assessment may in the future be categorized as an endocrine disruptor. Although its overall properties have been shown to be favorable as compared to its competitors, it would not be allowed onto the market.

Certain policymakers have claimed that the introduction of the hazard criteria will increase certainty, but in reality it will actually increase uncertainty and may well lead to a situation where newer and more benign chemicals are not being introduced into the market due to the new hazard-based hurdle in this new legislation.

Conclusion

The new directive has led to the loss in the availability of many active substances, and the new regulation includes additional measures, based on hazard "cutoff" criteria that are likely to further limit the availability of crop protection solutions for farmers. Moreover, the introduction of the hazard-based cutoff criteria moves away from a consideration of all risks to humans and the environment that may lead to the removal of chemicals that are important tools in agriculture and have excellent safety profiles.

The EU policy is not based on scientific advice, and the move toward politically driven criteria and away from risk assessment raises concerns about the future role of science and risk assessment in decision making, both in the EU and beyond.

Notes

1. The European Commission is the executive body of the European Union, and it is responsible for proposing legislation and managing new legislation following its adoption. For a copy of the progress report, see commission document reference COM(2001) 444 final, http://eur-lex.europa.eu/LexUriServ/LexUriServ.do?uri= COM:2001:0444:FIN:EN:PDF.

2. The Council of Ministers represents the governments of each of the EU member states, with decisions on this dossier taken by the Agricultural Council, made up of the agricultural ministers from each EU country. The European Parliament is made up of more than seven hundred Members of the European Parliament (MEPs), who are directly elected.

3. The majority of the active substances caught in this process did exhibit properties that are today listed as cut-off criteria.

4. The "Common position" is equivalent to a first legislative reading.

5. The Weybridge definition was agreed to in a European Commission workshop held in 1996. It states, "An endocrine disrupter is an exogenous substance that causes adverse health effects in an intact organism, or its progeny, secondary to changes in endocrine function."

6. From a commission press release of July 2006 announcing the adoption of the proposal for a new regulation, http://europa.eu/rapid/pressReleasesAction.do? reference=IP/06/982&format=HTML&aged=1&language=EN&guiLanguage=en).

7. Article 22(2) of Regulation 178/2002, http://eur-lex.europa.eu/LexUriServ/ LexUriServ.do?uri=CONSLEG:2002R0178:20060428:EN:PDF.

8. See, for example, the press release of June 2009 on MON810, http://www.efsa europa.eu/EFSA/efsa_locale-1178620753812_1211902628240.htm.

9. Letter from Commissioner Vassiliou to the European Crop Protection Association, 2009 (not publicly available).

10. See page 7 of European Commission proposal to amend cosmetics legislation, http://ec.europa.eu/enterprise/cosmetics/doc/com_2008_49/com_2008 _49_en.pdf.

11. Commissioner Barroso speech to the European Parliament, September 2009, http://europa.eu/rapid/pressReleasesAction.do?reference=SPEECH/09/391.

12. Communication from the Commission on the Precautionary Principle, February 2000, http://www.gdrc.org/u-gov/precaution-4.html.

13. UK statement in the Competitiveness Council, September 2009.

14. See report "How to Feed the World in 2050," http://www.fao.org/fileadmin/templates/wsfs/docs/expert_paper/How_to_Feed_the_World_in_2050.pdf.

2

The Problems with Precaution: A Principle without Principle

Jonathan H. Adler

It's better to be safe than sorry. We all accept this as a commonsense maxim. But can it also be a guiding principle for public policy? Advocates of the precautionary principle think so, and they argue that the formalization of a more "precautionary" approach to public health and environmental protection will better safeguard human well-being and the world around us. If only it were that easy.

Simply put, the precautionary principle is not a sound basis for public policy. Stated at the broadest level of generality, the principle is unobjectionable, but it provides no meaningful guidance to pressing policy questions. In a public policy context, "better safe than sorry" is a fairly vacuous instruction. Taken literally, the precautionary principle is either wholly arbitrary or incoherent. In its stronger formulations, the principle actually has the potential to be positively harmful.

Efforts to operationalize the precautionary principle into public law will do little to enhance the protection of public health and environmental protection. The precautionary principle could even do more harm than good. Efforts to impose the principle through regulatory policy inevitably accommodate competing concerns or become a Trojan horse for other ideological crusades. Selectively applied to politically disfavored technologies and conduct, the precautionary principle serves as a barrier to technological development and economic growth.

33

It is often sound policy to adopt precautionary measures in the face of uncertain or not wholly known health and environmental risks. Many existing environmental regulations adopt such an approach. Yet a broader application of the precautionary principle is not warranted and may actually undermine the goal its proponents claim to advance. In short, it could leave us more sorry and even less safe.

The Precautionary Principle Defined

According to its advocates, the precautionary principle traces its origins to the German principle of "foresight" or "forecaution"—*Vorsorgeprinzip.*[1] This principle formed the basis of social democratic environmental policies in West Germany, including measures to address the effects of acid precipitation on forests.[2] Germany was not alone, however, as other nations also adopted precautionary measures to address emerging environmental problems, as did various international bodies.[3]

The most common articulation of the precautionary principle is the Wingspread Statement on the Precautionary Principle, a consensus document drafted and adopted by a group of environmental activists and academics in January 1998.[4] The statement, which is reproduced in the appendix to this chapter, defined the precautionary principle in the following terms:

> When an activity raises threats of harm to human health or the environment, precautionary measures should be taken even if some cause and effect relationships are not fully established scientifically.

> In this context the proponent of an activity, rather than the public, should bear the burden of proof.

> The process of applying the Precautionary Principle must be open, informed and democratic and must include potentially affected parties. It must also involve an examination of the full range of alternatives, including no action.

Contrary to what its advocates claim, this principle does not provide a particularly useful, let alone prudent, guide to the development or implementation of environmental and public health measures. Taken literally, it does not even provide much guidance at all. Harvard law professor Cass Sunstein, who currently serves as the administrator of the Office of Information and Regulatory Affairs in the Obama administration, is particularly harsh in his assessment of the precautionary principle. According to Sunstein, "The precautionary principle, for all its rhetorical appeal, is deeply incoherent. It is of course true that we should take precautions against some speculative dangers. But there are always risks on both sides of a decision; inaction can bring danger, but so can action. Precautions, in other words, themselves create risks—and hence the principle bans what it simultaneously requires."[5]

The Wingspread Statement itself embodies many of the problems with the precautionary principle. The initial portion of the principle calls for something that is already done in the United States and other developed countries. Regulatory measures are routinely adopted when "some cause and effect relationships are not fully established scientifically." There is rarely, if ever, perfect certainty about the nature and causes of health and environmental threats, so environmental and public health regulations are almost always adopted despite the existence of some residual uncertainty.

American environmental law is filled with regulatory programs that authorize, or even compel, regulatory action in the absence of scientific certainty about the nature and extent of potential risks to the environment or public health. The Clean Air Act, for example, requires that the administrator of the Environmental Protection Agency (EPA) adopt measures to control various types of air pollution when, in the administrator's "judgment," the emission of certain pollutants "may reasonably be anticipated to endanger public health or welfare."[6] Absolute proof or scientific certainty is not required. Rather, a "reasonable" belief in the possibility of future harm is sufficient—indeed, such a belief may *require* action.[7] Other portions of the Clean Air Act require the EPA to set air quality standards at the level "requisite to protect the public health" with "an adequate margin of safety," irrespective of the cost.[8] Thus, the law requires the EPA to set the standard at a level more stringent than that which is known to threaten public health.

The Endangered Species Act also requires government action in the absence of scientific certainty. Under the Endangered Species Act, the Fish and Wildlife Service is to list species as endangered or threatened on the basis of the "best scientific and commercial data available."[9] That the "best available" scientific evidence may be inconclusive or uncertain does not relieve the Fish and Wildlife Service of its obligation to list a species if the "best available" evidence suggests that it could be threatened with extinction.

Federal environmental law also includes requirements that federal agencies consider the "full range of alternatives" and their likely environmental effects before taking action. Consider the National Environmental Policy Act, which requires the federal government to consider not only the likely environmental consequences of major federal actions but also various alternatives, including forgoing the proposed action altogether.[10] This would seem to line up nicely with the Wingspread Statement's call for "an examination of the full range of alternatives, including no action."

However precautionary these various regulatory measures may be, they are considered insufficient by most precautionary principle advocates. According to the Wingspread Statement, existing environmental regulations "have failed to protect adequately human health and the environment," and more is required. Those who signed the statement or point to it as a model for policy have not sought to defend existing laws so much as they have sought the adoption of environmental and other regulations that are more stringent. In the eyes of precautionary principle advocates, U.S. environmental regulations are too slow and inflexible, and insufficiently precautionary.[11]

The real teeth of the principle, as articulated in the Wingspread Statement, come from shifting the burden of proof to "the proponent of an activity." Here, "better safe than sorry" means that no activity that "raises threats of harm to human health or the environment" should proceed until it is proven "safe." Interpreted this way, the principle erects a potential barrier to any activity that could alter the status quo. Applied literally to all activities, it would be a recommendation for not doing anything of consequence, as all manner of activities "raise threats of harm to human health or the environment." As Sunstein observes, "Read for all its worth, it leads in no direction at all. The principle threatens to be paralyzing, forbidding regulation, inaction, and every step in between."[12]

Yet precautionary principle advocates rarely call for applying this principle neutrally across the board. Rather, they seek to impose this burden on private actors, most notably corporations, that propose altering the environmental landscape in some way or introducing a new product or technology into the stream of commerce. This creates an increased barrier to the adoption and implementation of new technologies and justifies lengthy approval programs and restrictions on technological advance.

An obvious question is why it is safer or more "precautionary" to focus on the potential harms of new activities or technologies without reference to the activities or technologies that they might displace. There is no a priori reason to assume that newer technologies or less known risks are more dangerous than older technologies or familiar threats. In many cases the exact opposite will be true. A new, targeted pesticide may pose fewer health and environmental risks than a pesticide developed ten, twenty, or thirty years ago. Shifting the burden of proof, as called for in the Wingspread Statement, is not a "precautionary" policy so much as it is a reactionary one. And as discussed below, this myopic focus on the threats posed by new activities or technologies can actually do more harm than good.

The last portion of the precautionary principle, with its focus on open decision making and information, does not appear to be focused much on "precaution" at all, but on transparency, accountability, and democratic consent. These are all important values in public policy, but there is no clear connection between these values and a more precautionary or risk-averse approach to public health and environmental policy. Affected communities, when informed about the relevant risks and trade-offs, may choose to accept certain environmental risks in return for economic or other benefits.

How this part of the principle operates in practice is contingent on how one defines "democratic" decision making and "potentially affected parties," and whether these values are allowed to conflict. Are the "potentially affected parties" those who are directly affected by the development of a technology or a given good or service? Or does any individual or interest group with a potential concern get to have their say too? In some cases, "democratizing" decisions about the acceptability of given technologies or marketplace transactions involves supplanting the decisions of those most involved through a political process. There is no guarantee this ensures adequate representation of those most affected or produces a more precautionary or environmentally protective result.[13]

The Precautionary Principle Abroad

The precautionary principle is not simply an idea promoted by activists and academics. The principle has found its way into a variety of legal instruments, including several international treaties. Although the principle has not yet reached the status of customary international law, it is increasingly common in international documents and statements of principle.

A soft articulation of the precautionary principle can be found in the Rio Declaration, adopted at the 1992 Earth Summit in Rio de Janeiro. It provides: "Where there are threats of serious or irreversible damage, lack of full scientific certainty shall not be used as a reason for postponing cost-effective measures to prevent environmental degradation."[14] This is a soft articulation because it does not apply to all innovations or all potential threats, but only those that pose "threats of serious or irreversible damage." It further embodies a measure of proportionality, as it only calls for the adoption of "cost-effective measures" to address such risks. Insofar as there are reasonable measures that can reduce an uncertain but serious risk, the Rio Declaration calls for action. As a consequence, it embodies a degree of proportionality.

A somewhat stronger formulation of the principle can be found in the preamble to the U.N. Convention on Biological Diversity. It similarly declares that "where there is a threat of significant reduction or loss of biological diversity, lack of full scientific certainty should not be used as a reason for postponing measures to avoid or minimize such a threat."[15]

A stronger formulation still is contained in the World Charter for Nature: "Where potential adverse effects are not fully understood, the activities should not proceed."[16] This is a reactionary and completely unworkable standard. Applied to technology it would bring technological progress to a halt, as there are always uncertain and unpredictable effects of new technologies. But this is not simply true of technology. All economic and social innovations have implications that are less than fully understood at the time they are adopted. The same goes for government policy. Indeed, were the

World Charter for Nature's formulation of the precautionary principle applied to governmental interventions in the economy, regulatory bureaucrats would forever sit on their hands, as centralized government decision makers never have complete knowledge or a full understanding of the likely effects of their policies.[17]

The 1992 Maastricht Treaty creating the European Union explicitly calls for the adoption of the precautionary principle in European environmental policy, even as it also urges consideration of the likely costs and benefits of specific measures. Article 130R(2) of the treaty provides:

> Community policy on the environment shall aim at a high level of protection taking into account the diversity of situations in the various regions of the Community. It shall be based on the precautionary principle and on the principles that preventive action should be taken, that environmental damage should as a priority be rectified at source and that the polluter should pay. Environmental protection requirements must be integrated into the definition and implementation of other Community policies.

Article 130R(3) further calls for the consideration of various factors in the development of environmental policy, including "available scientific and technical data" and "the potential benefits and costs of action or lack of action."[18]

Since the signing of the Maastricht Treaty, the precautionary principle has been incorporated into various aspects of European policy. Some nations have cited the principle as justification for prohibiting the use of hormones in livestock production or the importation of genetically modified crops. The European Council of Ministers adopted a formal resolution in April 1999 calling on the European Commission "to be in the future even more determined to be guided by the precautionary principle" in its legislative proposals.[19] This led to the European Commission's *Communication from the Commission on the Precautionary Principle*, which declared that the EU would apply the precautionary principle "where preliminary objective scientific evaluation indicates that there are reasonable grounds for concern that the potentially dangerous effects on the environment, human, animal, or plant health may be inconsistent with the high level of protection chosen for the community."[20] The resulting policies have created what some characterize as a "guilty until proven innocent" approach to the approval of new products.[21]

Precautionary principle advocates often point to EU environmental policies as better exemplars of precautionary policy than U.S. regulations. As Joel Tickner and Carolyn Raffensperger explain, "European decision-makers have no pressure to justify what are essentially political decisions in the artificially rational language of science or economics."[22] Critics likewise note that the EU appears to use precautionary rhetoric about environmental threats to defend decisions that appear more motivated by economic or cultural concerns, such as the preservation of small farms and rural communities across the European countryside. The precautionary principle seems to be invoked against some risks and not against others.[23] Even in Europe, it is difficult to maintain that the precautionary principle provides the foundation for safety or health-enhancing policies.

Is Precaution Safer than the Alternatives?

The biggest problem with the precautionary principle is that it does not clearly enhance the protection of public health and the environment. As University of Texas law professor Frank Cross observes, "The truly fatal flaw of the precautionary principle, ignored by almost all the commentators, is the unsupported presumption that an action aimed at public health protection cannot possibly have negative effects on public health."[24] In any risk policy decision, policymakers can make two potential errors. On the one hand, policymakers may err by failing to adopt measures to address a health or environmental risk that exists. On the other hand, policymakers may adopt regulatory measures to control a health or environmental risk that does not exist. Both types of error can result in increased risks to public health.

Regulatory drug approval, as conducted by the Food and Drug Administration, provides a good example of how both types of error can increase net risks to public health. The FDA must approve new drugs before they may be used or prescribed. FDA approval is fairly precautionary, as it will only approve those drugs that are shown to be "safe and effective." This standard is designed to prevent the release of an unsafe drug. Delaying the availability of potentially lifesaving treatment, however, poses risks of its own. In the simplest terms, if a new drug or medical treatment will start saving lives once it is approved, then the longer it takes for the government to approve the drug, the more likely it is that people will die awaiting treatment.[25]

The negative consequences of failing to quickly approve a lifesaving drug can be quite significant. Consider the example of Misoprostol, a drug that prevents gastric ulcers.[26] Misoprostol was developed in the early 1980s and was first approved in some nations in 1985. The FDA, however, did not approve use of Misoprostol until 1988. Even though the drug was already available in several dozen foreign countries, the FDA subjected Misoprostol to a nine-and-one-half-month review. At the time, between ten thousand and twenty thousand people died of gastric ulcers per year. Had Misoprostol been approved more rapidly, it could have saved as many as eight thousand to fifteen thousand lives. Thus, in seeking to prevent one risk—the risk of approving an unsafe drug—the FDA contributed to the risk of gastric ulcers by preventing the use of a potentially lifesaving drug.

If the goal is to have a drug approval process that maximizes the protection of public health, the risks of premature drug approval need to be weighed against the risks of failing to approve new medications rapidly enough. In this context, the precautionary principle, and in particular the burden-shifting framework advocated by its proponents, cannot be assumed to result in greater protection of public health and the environment. In fact, as the experience with the FDA drug approval process in the United States shows, a more precautionary approach could do more harm than good. Whether or not one accepts this indictment of the FDA drug approval process, the underlying lesson is clear: Increased precaution does not come without potential costs to the very values precaution is supposed to protect.

Precaution and Pesticides

The same balancing of risks that is necessary in the drug approval context must be used in the case of agricultural chemicals if the goal is to maximize the protection of public health and the environment. Just as there are two possible types of errors that can be made in the drug approval process, there are two types of errors that can be made in the regulation of agricultural chemicals. On the one hand, policymakers may fail to control adequately the pesticides and other chemicals that pose a significant risk to public health or the environment. On the other hand, regulations may prevent or discourage the use of agricultural chemicals that could enhance human welfare and even enhance the protection of public health and the environment.

Pesticides and other agricultural chemicals may present many different risks. Exposure or consumption of agricultural chemicals may pose a direct threat to human health. Misuse of such chemicals can also contaminate water supplies, disrupt ecosystems, and harm other animal and plant species.

The risks posed by improper or excessive use of agricultural chemicals are serious, but they do not justify precautionary regulation, as there are countervailing risks from the excess regulation of agricultural chemicals. In particular, limits on the use of agricultural chemicals may lower crop yields, which may require the planting of more acreage or an increase in prices for agricultural products. Making fresh fruits and vegetables more expensive may have negative human health impacts as consumers substitute other, less healthy foods. Reductions in crop productivity can have serious environmental effects, including the loss of species habitat and consequent effects on biodiversity. If precautionary controls are imposed only on the adoption or introduction of new agricultural chemicals, this may result in the continued use of less safe or less effective compounds, thereby enhancing the very risks precautionary regulation is meant to avoid.

The fungicide ethylene dibromide (EDB) illustrates the risk-risk nature of agricultural chemicals. EDB was used to control mold on grains, but was restricted in 1983 due to fears that it was a potential carcinogen. Yet molds themselves can be a source of carcinogens in the human diet.[27] Perhaps more important, the agricultural chemicals that replaced EDB were less effective and were used in higher quantities, increasing the risk for exposed workers.[28] Thus, while the regulation of EDB reduced certain risks, it also led to an increase in others. The only way to know whether the regulation of EDB increased the protection of public health and the environment is to compare these risks and weigh them against each other.

The environmental risks of forgoing advances in agricultural technologies are particularly severe. Global food demand is increasing dramatically, in part due to increases in global population. By 2050 there could be nearly nine billion mouths to feed worldwide.

It will not be enough for food production and distribution to keep up with increases in population, however. Approximately eight hundred million people receive inadequate nutrition in their diets at present, and more than six million children die annually of malnutrition. If agricultural productivity were held at 1997 levels, the world would need to put more than 1.5 billion hectares under plow to meet increased demand. Yet if agricultural productivity increases by as little as 1 percent a year from 1997 through 2050, that figure drops to an estimated 325 million hectares. If agricultural productivity could increase at a rate of 1.5 percent, it is possible we could return nearly one hundred million hectares from agriculture to nature.[29] Limiting the development and introduction of new agricultural chemicals will make this task only more difficult. Applying a precautionary regulatory regime to agricultural chemicals could have serious environmental consequences.

Wealthier Is Healthier and Richer Is Cleaner

Advocates of the precautionary principle tend to assume that economic growth and development are themselves a threat to public health and environmental protection. The Wingspread Statement, for example, speaks of the "substantial unintended consequences" brought about by industrialization.[30] An underlying premise of the precautionary principle is that modern industrial society is unsustainable and threatens the survival of humanity, if not much of the planet as well. This assumption is highly questionable.[31] Economic growth and technological progress have been a tremendous boon to both human health and environmental protection. Efforts to limit such progress are likely to be counterproductive. Regulatory measures that stifle innovation and suppress economic growth will deprive individuals of the resources necessary to improve their quality of life and deny societies the ability to make investments that protect people and their environs.

The rise of modern industrial society produced an explosion of potential health and environmental risks, but it also generated a vast degree of wealth and technological advance that led to unprecedented improvements in public health. For centuries, average life expectancy was scarcely more than a few decades. In 1900, U.S. life expectancy was less than fifty years.[32] Today, however, U.S. life expectancy is approaching eighty years.[33] Similar advances have been observed in other nations as they have developed.[34] Infant and maternal mortality rates have plummeted over the past century, as have the incidence and mortality rates of typhoid, diphtheria, tuberculosis, and numerous other diseases.[35] These positive trends are largely the result of increased wealth and the benefits such wealth brings. Higher economic growth and aggregate wealth strongly correlate with reduced mortality and morbidity.[36] This should be no surprise, as the accumulation of wealth is necessary to fund medical research, support markets for advanced lifesaving technologies, and build infrastructure necessary for better food distribution, and so on. In a phrase, poorer is sicker, and wealthier is healthier.[37]

Economic progress is no less essential for environmental protection than for protection of public health. Environmental protection is a good, and, like all goods, it must be purchased. Wealth is required to finance environmental improvements, from the purification of drinking water and control of raw sewage to the development of cleaner combustion technologies and low-emission modes of transport. Wealthier societies have both the means and the desire to address a wider array of environmental concerns and improve the protection of public health.[38] Economic growth fuels technological advances and generates the resources necessary to deploy new methods for meeting human needs efficiently and effectively. Public support for environmental measures, both public and private, is correlated with changes in personal income.[39]

Pollution, although still a serious environmental problem in much of the world, is not the mortal threat to human survival it once was. A century ago, soot and smoke permeated cities, sometimes to lethal effect. In 1948, a four-day weather inversion in Donora, Pennsylvania, blanketed the town with pollution from local factories, killing eighteen people.[40] River fires, such as those that brought infamy to the Cuyahoga, were a relatively common occurrence on industrial waterways in the late nineteenth and early twentieth centuries.[41] Over the past several decades, pollution levels in wealthy, industrialized societies have declined, particularly in the case of those emissions for which the health impacts are most severe.[42] As environmental analyst Indur Goklany observes,

"Countries undergo an environmental transition as they become wealthier and reach a point at which they start getting cleaner."[43] This occurs first with particularly acute environmental concerns, such as access to safe drinking water and sanitation services. As affluence increases, so does the attention paid to conventional pollution concerns, such as fecal coliform bacteria and urban air quality.[44]

New technologies pose risks, to be sure. This is as true for agricultural and industrial chemicals as it is for anything else. Without question, some of the chemicals and other technologies targeted by advocates of the precautionary principle can cause problems if misused. Yet it is notable that the proliferation of these technologies has coincided with the greatest explosion of prosperity and longevity in human history. If modern society were as risky as precautionary principle advocates suggest, this should not be the case.

Precaution's Appeal

If the precautionary principle is not a useful guide to sound public health and environmental policy, then what explains its appeal? The rhetoric of prudence and caution is no doubt appealing to many, but there is also something more. Traditional formulations of the precautionary principle reinforce certain common cognitive biases. At the same time, the principle provides a convenient vehicle for those who seek to advance more contro versial ideological or economically motivated policies.

Sunstein has identified several cognitive biases that reinforce the precautionary principle's appeal. These include loss aversion, the myth of a benevolent nature, the availability heuristic, probability neglect, and system neglect.[45] In a variety of ways, the precautionary principle reinforces people's natural preference for risk avoidance and the fact that most people "dislike losses far more than they like corresponding gains."[46] Most people also have a difficult time recognizing or accounting for the actual probability of a given event or the nature of trade-offs across risks. At the same time, many people have a particularly "benign" view of nature and the natural world, particularly when compared to modern technology, and people generally tend to focus on those risks that are cognitively "available" at the exclusion of other risks that may be less transparent or clear. As a consequence, sensational and unusual risk may command public attention and generate the demand for a policy response, even at great cost, while larger, more mundane risks remain largely ignored. Precautionary rhetoric feeds on, and is fed by, these concerns.

Sunstein is almost certainly correct that such cognitive biases reinforce the precautionary principle's appeal, but there is likely more to the story. The precautionary principle provides a convenient vehicle for those who seek to advance ideological or economic interests in the context of public health or environmental policy. Those who seek to block the development of agricultural biotechnology or reduce the use of chemicals will have limited success with a direct appeal. Couching their opposition in the language of prudence and precaution, however, may help them advance the ball. Presented in such terms, technology-limiting policies appear less radical or disruptive and may garner greater public support.

Economic interests also have reason to adopt precautionary appeals insofar as such appeals enable these groups to erect barriers to competing technologies or firms, close off markets, or otherwise use environmental regulations as a tool for rent seeking. There is a long and sordid history of corporations and industries using environmental regulations for their own private material gain.[47] Insofar as these groups seek to prevent market competition, precautionary rhetoric may be particularly valuable. This is especially evident in the trade context, where international trade rules limit the ability of nations to close off their markets to goods from abroad, but still allow the adoption of trade barriers with a legitimate health or environmental pedigree. Thus, the EU has resisted imports of hormone-treated beef and agricultural biotechnology with claims that their safety has not yet been proved, even though there is substantial reason to believe that economic interests are the underlying motivation.

In Search of Safety

Can the precautionary principle provide any sort of useful guide for health and environmental policy? Goklany has proposed a set of tiered criteria that could be used to operationalize the precautionary principle in a health- and safety-enhancing manner.[48] In his framework, greater attention should be paid to identified risks to human mortality and morbidity, for example, than to less certain or immediate environmental threats. His framework may well provide a more effective way to ensure that precautionary policies have a truly precautionary effect, but it clearly does not produce the results most principle advocates defend. As applied by Goklany, for example, the precautionary principle would counsel against many restrictions on the use of DDT and agricultural biotechnology, and it would not support drastic measures to address the threat of climate change.

Whether or not Goklany's framework presents the best way forward, one thing should be abundantly clear: True precaution requires recognizing that risks trade off against other risks. The risks of new technologies have to be weighed against the risks of doing without. The harms of environmental disruptions must be weighed against the consequences of merely preserving the status quo.

The stated aim of the precautionary principle is to enhance protection of public health and environmental concerns. In practice, however, the precautionary principle is only applied to the risks of technological change and industrial society, with little appreciation for the risks that wealth and technology prevent. New technologies can be risky things. Some industrial chemicals may cause health problems even if used carefully. But this does not justify the adoption of a blanket precautionary rule suppressing chemical use and technological development.

If the true aim is a safer world, and not merely the restriction of industrial activity for its own sake or the retardation of technological progress, the risks of new chemicals or products must be weighed against the risks that they ameliorate or prevent. The risks of change must be weighed against the risk of stagnation. In every case, "the empirical question is whether the health [and environmental] gains from the regulation of the substances involved are greater or lesser than the health [and environmental] costs of the regulation."[40]

While the advocates of the precautionary principle rely on the rhetoric of prudence and public health protection, they encourage the exclusive focus on one set of risks while ignoring others. Contrary to what your mother may have told you, "better safe than sorry" isn't always safer. In fact, when it comes to policies to protect public health and the environment, this type of thinking could do us in.

Appendix to Chapter 2

The Wingspread Statement
on the Precautionary Principle

The release and use of toxic substances, the exploitation of resources, and physical alterations of the environment have had substantial unintended consequences affecting human health and the environment. Some of these concerns are high rates of learning deficiencies, asthma, cancer, birth defects and species extinctions; along with global climate change, stratospheric ozone depletion and worldwide contamination with toxic substances and nuclear materials.

We believe existing environmental regulations and other decisions, particularly those based on risk assessment, have failed to protect adequately human health and the environment—the larger system of which humans are but a part.

We believe there is compelling evidence that damage to humans and the worldwide environment is of such magnitude and seriousness that new principles for conducting human activities are necessary.

While we realize that human activities may involve hazards, people must proceed more carefully than has been the case in recent history. Corporations, government entities, organizations, communities, scientists and other individuals must adopt a precautionary approach to all human endeavors.

Therefore, it is necessary to implement the Precautionary Principle: When an activity raises threats of harm to human health or the environment, precautionary measures should be taken even if some cause and effect relationships are not fully established scientifically.

In this context the proponent of an activity, rather than the public, should bear the burden of proof.

The process of applying the Precautionary Principle must be open, informed and democratic and must include potentially affected parties. It must also involve an examination of the full range of alternatives, including no action.

Notes

1. Carolyn Raffensperger and Joel Tickner, "Introduction: To Foresee and Forestall," in *Protecting Public Health and the Environment: Implementing the Precautionary Principle* (Washington, DC: Island Press, 1999), 4.

2. Ibid.; Andrew Jordan and Timothy O'Riordan, "The Precautionary Principle in Contemporary Environmental Policy and Politics," in *Protecting Public Health and the Environment*, 19.

3. For an overview of the incorporation of the precautionary principle in various international instruments, see Julian Morris, "Defining the Precautionary Principle," in *Rethinking Risk and the Precautionary Principle*, ed. Julian Morris (Woburn, MA: Butterworth-Heinemann, 2000).

4. See "Wingspread Statement on the Precautionary Principle," Science and Environmental Health Network, http://www.sehn.org/wing.html.

5. Cass R. Sunstein, "Throwing Precaution to the Wind: Why the 'Safe' Choice Can Be Dangerous," *Boston Globe*, July 13, 2008. For a more extensive critique, see Cass R. Sunstein, *The Laws of Fear: Beyond the Precautionary Principle* (Cambridge: Cambridge University Press, 2005).

6. See, for example, 42 U.S.C. §7521(a)(1), which provides in relevant part: "The Administrator shall by regulation prescribe (and from time to time revise) in accordance with the provisions of this section, standards applicable to the emission of any air pollutant from any class or classes of new motor vehicles or new motor vehicle engines, which in his judgment cause, or contribute to, air pollution which may reasonably be anticipated to endanger public health or welfare." Other provisions in the Clean Air Act contain similar requirements.

7. See, for example, *Natural Resources Defense Council, Inc. v. Train*, 411 F.Supp. 864 (S.D.N.Y. 1976).

8. See 42 U.S.C. §7409(b)(1), which provides in relevant part: "National primary ambient air quality standards, prescribed under subsection (a) of this section shall be ambient air quality standards the attainment and maintenance of which in the judgment of the Administrator, based on such criteria and allowing an adequate margin of safety, are requisite to protect the public health. Such primary standards may be revised in the same manner as promulgated." As interpreted by

the Supreme Court, this language precludes considering costs when setting the standards. *Whitman v. American Trucking Associations*, 531 U.S. 457 (2001).

9. See 16 U.S.C. §1533.

10. See 42 U.S.C. §4332.

11. See, for example, Joel Tickner and Carolyn Raffensperger, "The Politics of Precaution in the United States and the European Union," *Global Environmental Change* 11 (2001): 175, 177.

12. Sunstein, *Laws of Fear*, 14.

13. For an extended discussion of why expanding the range of potentially affected parties who have standing to challenge environmental harms may not improve environmental protection, see Jonathan H. Adler, "Stand or Deliver? Citizen Suits, Standing, and Environmental Protection," *Duke Environmental Law and Public Policy Forum* 12, no. 1 (2001): 39–83.

14. Rio Declaration on Environment and Development, UN Conference on Environment and Development, UN Doc. A/CONF.151/5/Rev.1 (1992).

15. United Nations Convention on Biological Diversity, June 5, 1992, preamble.

16. World Charter for Nature, G.A. Res. 37/7, UN GAOR, 37th Sess., Supp. No. 51, at section (II)(11)(b), UN Doc. A/Res/37/7 (1992).

17. As Nobel laureate economist F. A. Hayek observed, "The knowledge of the circumstances of which we must make use never exists in concentrated or integrated form but solely as the dispersed bits of incomplete and frequently contradictory knowledge which all the separate individuals possess." F. A. Hayek, "The Use of Knowledge in Society," *American Economic Review* 35, no. 4 (1945): 519–30.

18. Treaty on European Union, February 7, 1992, 1992 O.J. (C 191) 1, art. 130R(3).

19. European Commission, *Communication from the Commission on the Precautionary Principle* (Brussels: Commission of the European Communities, 2000), 7.

20. Ibid., 9–10.

21. See Tim Lougheed, "Understanding the Role of Science in Regulation," *Environmental Health Perspectives* 117, no. 3 (March 2009): A109.

22. Tickner and Raffensperger, "Politics of Precaution," 178.

23. See Jonathan Weiner and Michael Rogers, "Comparing Precaution in the United States and Europe," *Journal of Risk Research* 5 (2002): 317–49.

24. Frank B. Cross, "Paradoxical Perils of the Precautionary Principle," *Washington and Lee Law Review* 53, no. 3 (1996): 860.

25. Sam Kazman, "Deadly Overcaution: FDA's Drug Approval Process," *Journal of Regulation and Social Costs* (September 1990): 35.

26. This discussion is based on the Kazman article; ibid., 47–48.

27. George M. Gray and John D. Graham, "Regulating Pesticides," in *Risk versus Risk: Tradeoffs in Protecting Health and the Environment*, ed. John D. Graham and Jonathan Baert Weiner (Cambridge, MA: Harvard University Press, 1995), 186–87.

28. Cross, "Paradoxical Perils," 875–76.

29. Indur M. Goklany, *The Precautionary Principle: A Critical Appraisal of Environmental Risk Assessment* (Washington, DC: Cato Institute, 2001), 31–32.

30. Raffensperger and Tickner, Appendix A, *Protecting Public Health and the Environment*, 353–55.

31. For a contrary view, see Bjorn Lomborg, *The Skeptical Environmentalist: Measuring the Real State of the World* (Cambridge: Cambridge University Press, 2001). For critical consideration of Lomborg's thesis, see the symposium "The Virtues and Vices of Skeptical Environmentalism," *Case Western Reserve Law Review* 53, no. 2 (2002).

32. "United States Life Tables," *National Vital Statistics Reports* 56, no. 9 (December 28, 2007): table 11.

33. According to the U.S. Centers for Disease Control and Prevention, life expectancy at birth was 77.7 in 2006. Melonie Heron et al., "Deaths: Final Data for 2006," *National Vital Statistics Reports* 57, no. 14 (April 17, 2009): 1.

34. See Nicholas Eberstadt, "Population, Food, and Income: Global Trends in the Twentieth Century," in *The True State of the Planet*, ed. Ronald Bailey (New York: Free Press, 1995), 21–26.

35. Ibid.

36. See, for example, Susan L. Ettner, "New Evidence on the Relationship between Income and Health," *Journal of Health Economics* 15 (1996): 67; John D. Graham et al., "Poorer Is Riskier," *Risk Analysis* 12, no. 3 (1992): 333–37; Ralph L. Keeney, "Mortality Risks Induced by Economic Expenditures," *Risk Analysis* 10, no. 1 (1990): 147–59.

37. This phrasing is attributed to the late Aaron Wildavsky.

38. See Goklany, *Precautionary Principle*, 22–24, 75 79.

39. See Matthew E. Kahn and John G. Matsusaka, "Demand for Environmental Goods: Evidence from Voting Patterns on California Initiatives," *Journal of Law and Economics* 40, no. 1 (1997).

40. Cited in Indur M. Goklany, "Richer Is Cleaner," in *True State of the Planet*, 347.

41. See Jonathan H. Adler, "Fables of the Cuyahoga: Reconstructing a History of Environmental Protection," *Fordham Environmental Law Journal* 14, no, 1 (2002): 89–146.

42. See Indur Goklany, *Clearing the Air: The Real Story of the War on Air Pollution* (Washington, DC: Cato Institute, 1999).

43. Goklany, "Richer Is Cleaner," 339, 341.

44. Goklany observes that although the "environmental transition" for drinking water and sanitation occurs "almost immediately as the level of affluence increases above subsistence," the transition appears to occur at approximately $1,375 per capita for fecal coliform and $3,280 and $3,670 per capita for urban particulate matter and sulfur dioxide concentrations respectively. Ibid., 342. For a fuller treatment of the correlation between affluence and air quality, see Goklany, *Clearing the Air*.

45. See Cass R. Sunstein, "Beyond the Precautionary Principle," John M. Olin Law and Economics Working Paper No. 149, University of Chicago Law School, January 2003.

46. Ibid.

47. See Jonathan H. Adler, "Rent Seeking behind the Green Curtain," *Regulation* 19, no. 4 (1999). See also Michael S. Greve and Fred L. Smith, Jr., eds., *Environmental Politics: Public Costs, Private Rewards* (New York: Praeger, 1992); and Terry L. Anderson, ed., *Political Environmentalism: Going behind the Green Curtain* (Palo Alto, CA: Hoover Press, 2000).

48. See Goklany, *Precautionary Principle*, 8–11.

49. Aaron Wildavsky, *But Is It True?* (Cambridge, MA: Harvard University Press, 1995), 428.

PART II

Case Studies

3

The Case of Atrazine

Jon Entine

Farmers have been known to say that the two most important inventions in the history of agriculture have been the plow and atrazine. The odorless white powder is applied on farms to control a broad range of yield-robbing grassy weeds. In the agricultural world, the herbicide is considered almost a miracle chemical. In combination with other products, it can help boost the efficacy of other weed killers. It was among the first of what are called "selective herbicides" that destroy weeds that would otherwise choke a crop and starve it of nutrients but do not harm the crop itself. It is considered so comparatively gentle by farmers that it can be applied even after the first shoots appear above the ground.

Manufactured by the Swiss agrichemical company Syngenta, and licensed in the United States since 1958, atrazine is part of the chemical family of triazine herbicides used on many fruits and vegetables, including nuts, citrus, and grapes. Almost half of it is applied in the United States, where it is used on dozens of crops, including more than half of corn, 90 percent of sugar cane, and two-thirds of sorghum. More than 160 million pounds of its active ingredient are produced annually. Although regulatory agencies have consistently determined that atrazine is safe as used, it has come under relentless attack by advocacy groups and some university scientists convinced that it poses serious health problems for marine animals and, by extension, to humans. They warn that it affects human reproduction and hormonal activity, making it equivalent to a ticking chemical time bomb.

Atrazine fits a variety of farming systems. It is credited as being a key factor in the transformation of farming from the relatively low-yield, massively labor-intensive activity that prevailed into the first half of the twentieth century and through the Dust Bowl thirties into the advanced, high-technology industry it has become today. It is the most widely used herbicide in conservation tillage systems, which are designed to prevent soil erosion. It has become a critical tool in the no-plow revolution that is helping to cut carbon pollution.

Herbicides conserve water because the stalks, husks, and other crop residue from previous harvests are left on the ground and the soil is not plowed up. Less plowing means less use of oil-hungry farm machinery. Not turning over the earth to kill weeds also keeps huge amounts of carbon dioxide trapped in the ground, limiting CO_2 emissions. According to the U.S. Department of Energy, if no-till and other conservation methods were more widely adopted, carbon emissions could be reduced by billions of tons a year—savings mitigating much of the carbon released from fossil fuels each year.[1]

Some analysts estimate that 10 to 40 percent of sugar cane yield could be lost if atrazine were banned. An EPA study concluded that it boosts yields by 6 percent or more, saving corn farmers as much as $28 per acre—more than $2 billion in direct economic benefits, which could be the difference between staying solvent and going bankrupt for many. The report added that if atrazine were unavailable to corn farmers, the "yield loss plus increased herbicide cost may result in an average estimated loss of $28 per acre."[2] Another study looking at combined data from 236 university cornfield trials from 1986 to 2005 found that crops treated with atrazine yielded an average of 5.7 bushels more per acre than those treated with alternative herbicides.[3]

Not everyone agrees with those estimates, however. Harvard economist Frank Ackerman, who has campaigned for tighter restrictions on atrazine and other chemicals and works closely with advocacy critics, wrote a controversial analysis in 2007 challenging the EPA study, claiming atrazine increases yields by as little as 1 percent.[4]

Studies and Regulation

Atrazine is one of the most assessed and regulated agricultural chemicals in history. There have been more than six thousand studies on the herbicide, compared to the one hundred to two hundred safety studies generally required by the U.S. Environmental Protection Agency before registering a product. It has long been considered safe because it has a short half-life, negligibly accumulates in organisms, and reportedly induces abnormalities and deformities only at very high doses.[5]

Under stringent international standards, atrazine has been approved as safe in regulatory reviews throughout the world. No country has ever discontinued the use of atrazine based on evidence of health dangers—including the member states of the European Union, where it is now banned. In 1996, when the EU formally evaluated atrazine, its reviews were positive: "It is expected that the use of atrazine, consistent with good plant protection practice, will not have any harmful effects on human or animal health or any unacceptable effects on the environment," the regulators concluded.[6] However, faced with arguments that there were lingering uncertainties about the "hidden dangers" of chemicals, officials refocused on the unknown potential for harm rather than evidence of harm. In 2003 the EU committee reviewing atrazine confirmed traces of it in groundwater. Although the levels were not known to pose a safety risk, the review undertaken under the precautionary principle led to a regulatory ban, which went into effect in 2005.[7]

Other regulatory bodies, even those that incorporate precautionary standards, have decided there is no justification for a ban. In 2004 Canada, which has restricted other controversial chemicals such as bisphenol A (the ubiquitous additive used in plastic bottles and metal can liners), determined it is safe.[8] The World Health Organization (WHO) and the Food and Agriculture Organization of the United Nations concluded in 2007 that atrazine is not teratogenic (does not cause malformations of an embryo or a fetus).[9] After an extensive re-review of atrazine in 2008, the Australian government concluded that it "continues to be satisfied that [atrazine] can be safely used in Australia, subject to those conditions outlined on product labels."[10] (Faced with a claim in 2010 by one researcher that atrazine may be associated with birth defects, the Australian government again reviewed the data and again concluded its safety designation was appropriate. It wrote on its "Chemicals in the News" Web site: "Every year, a number of epidemiological studies describing correlations between certain human health or environmental findings and pesticide use are published. Because of the relatively low rate of occurrence of birth defects, epidemiological studies of this type offer some useful information and hypotheses. In the regulatory context, any causal link has to be established by more extensive investigations and targeted follow-up studies."[11])

Atrazine has faced the most intense scrutiny in the United States, where it has been almost continuously evaluated for decades. In 1988 Congress directed the EPA to review atrazine, along with nearly nine hundred other pesticides. Over the next two decades, the agency generated more than a million pages of documents on atrazine. Although regulatory authorities and scientists who rely on long-established study protocols had consistently concluded that atrazine presents no serious harm as utilized, aggressive campaigns by advocacy groups, such as the Natural Resources Defense Council (NRDC), the Environmental Working Group (EWG), and the Pesticide Action Network (PAN) prompted another review in 2005. After one of the most intense analyses of any substance in history, the EPA formally relicensed it in 2006, declaring atrazine safe when properly used.

Ban proponents, emboldened by the EU ban, did not give up, however. The NRDC had sued the EPA in 2004 under provisions of several federal laws that the advocacy group claimed should have long ago led to a ban, but it lost. After the Obama administration took office in 2009, the NRDC saw an opening to again press its case. In August of that year, it issued a scathing, well-publicized critique, accusing the agency of ignoring the presence of atrazine in drinking water and in natural watersheds across the Midwest.[12]

The media gave the report enormous attention, reinvigorating advocacy blogs and stirring politicians. In October 2009—barely three years after the EPA had completed one of the most exhaustive scientific investigations of a commercial product ever undertaken and had reauthorized its use—the agency announced it would reevaluate atrazine once again, citing the NRDC report as its reason. "Our examination of atrazine will be based on transparency and sound science, including independent scientific peer review," said Steve Owens, head of the Office of Prevention, Pesticides and Toxic Substances, in an implicit swipe at the Bush administration, which had a reputation for playing politics with controversial scientific issues.[13] The EPA subsequently convened a series of "scientific advisory panels" (SAPs), comprised of yet another team of independent scientists, to reexamine the chemical on an accelerated schedule.

Harm versus Risk

There is no question that agricultural chemicals sometimes make their way into streams and water supplies. Atrazine is one of many hundreds of compounds that can be detected in water. Every year hundred of thousands of pounds of the herbicide become airborne and fall with rain, sometimes hundreds of miles from the source. Although atrazine breaks down quickly when exposed to air, it has been detected in infinitesimal levels—measured in parts per billion (ppb)—in lakes, streams, and other waterways and in drinking-water systems in agricultural areas.

Does atrazine at the residue levels found in drinking water in the United States, Europe, and elsewhere pose harm to humans, as is sometimes reported? The controversy revolves around perceptions of chemicals and risk. The mere presence of a compound in water does not mean there is a threat to human health. The EPA has strict standards to monitor the presence of trace chemicals to ensure that water supplies are safe. Scientists have long used what is called a "weight of evidence" approach to assess potential toxicity, which requires balancing complex and often conflicting evidence. They attempt to discover at what exposures a chemical might harm an animal and then set human exposure levels tens of thousands of times lower. This built-in safety cushion ensures that no one is overexposed. This is the high-threshold standard used by the EPA and regulatory bodies to assess atrazine.

The gap between the public's perception of harm and scientific determinations of risk is often large. A 2008 investigation by the Associated Press found an array of pharmaceuticals in the drinking water of 41 million Americans. That story touched off a panic of sorts among New Yorkers, proud of their pristine drinking water, and prompted a study by the city that indeed found traces of chemicals—but at levels measured in the parts per trillion (ppt).[14] One ppt is equivalent to one drop of water in twenty-six Olympic-size swimming pools, officials noted.[15]

The exposure levels set by regulatory bodies for the annual average concentration of a chemical are somewhat arbitrary. In the case of atrazine and all agricultural chemicals, the EU cutoff is 1 ppb. The U.S. cutoff (set by the EPA based on its former, erroneous, and since-revised determination that atrazine was a carcinogen) is 3 ppb, Canada's is 5 ppb, the United Kingdom's is 15 ppb, and Australia's is 40 ppb. In October 2010, after reviewing various international standards and the latest scientific data, the World Health Organization concluded that these policies are all far too restrictive, revising its standard to 100 ppb.[16]

On occasion, atrazine has been detected in drinking water at very low concentrations close to the EPA limit. A 2006 U. S. Geological Survey found approximately 75 percent of stream water and 40 percent of groundwater samples from selected agricultural areas in the Midwest contained traces of atrazine that occasionally spiked over 3 ppb.[17] Some NGOs publicized the report as evidence of atrazine's dangers. But that is not what the study suggested.

The EPA's 3 ppb limit is considered one thousand times safer than a level shown to have no health effects in the most sensitive species of laboratory animals. To put this in perspective using EPA data, it is estimated that even if a person were to drink thousands of gallons of water containing 3 ppb of atrazine every day for decades, he or she would still not drink amounts shown to have effects in lab studies. Said another way, the 2006 survey found miniscule erosion of the huge safety cushion. Using the standards in place in Canada, the UK, Australia, or under the new WHO guidelines, the concerns expressed by NGOs seem extreme.

Under an agreement with the EPA, Syngenta conducts weekly testing during the growing season of any drinking-water system with annual atrazine levels above 2.6 ppb. The already low levels of the herbicide found in water have been trending downward over the last fifteen years. According to the EPA, concentrations in raw water declined significantly between 1994 and 2006 at 103 frequently monitored sites.[18]

However, in its 2009 report, the NRDC crunched the raw EPA data and found that three local water systems—two in Illinois and one in Indiana—in previous years, on occasion, temporarily had exceeded the 3 ppb

EPA limit (which already incorporates a 1,000-fold safety cushion) by fractional amounts. The EPA was aware of the occasional spikes—its regulations permit these as inevitable—but does not consider them a safety threat. The NRDC, however, characterized the findings as "particularly alarming," asserting that "potential adverse effects [are] associated with even short exposures to atrazine"[19]—an opinion that, while sensational and widely circulated by a credulous media, has not been confirmed in any study or accepted by the EPA.

Steve Bradbury, deputy director in the Office of Pesticide Programs at the EPA, said the monitoring program has never found atrazine levels approaching the ninety-day or one-day maximums.[20] A cumulative risk assessment for triazine pesticides (the family of chemicals that includes atrazine) published by the EPA in 2006 concluded, "Risk assessments for cumulative exposures to triazine residues via drinking water based on currently registered uses of atrazine and simazine are not of concern."[21]

The "Endocrine Disruptor Low Dose" Hypothesis Controversy

Atrazine's comparatively benign toxicological profile has long posed a challenge for its critics. Tyrone Hayes, a University of California herpetologist (research focus on amphibians), is the most ardent. The Berkeley professor began studying atrazine in the 1990s with research funded by Syngenta, as part of its due diligence. Hayes and the company parted ways in the late 1990s. He maintains that he came to suspect that atrazine was interfering with the natural production of hormones and decided to pursue his research independently.

In 2002, Hayes published a study that ban proponents had been hoping for. His team focused on amphibian populations, which have been in worldwide decline for decades, baffling scientists. In lab experiments that exposed clawed frogs to lower doses of atrazine, the researchers produced males with ambiguous genitalia and squeaky, soprano-like croaks—hermaphrodites. "We hypothesize that atrazine induces aromatase [a protein that spurs the production of the female hormone estrogen] and promotes the conversion of testosterone to estrogen," the Hayes team wrote.[22]

Hayes's study set off an immediate firestorm. It was released at the same time as another team, part of a much larger study funded by Syngenta but also operating independently, was finding no meaningful link between atrazine exposure and abnormalities. Keith Solomon of the University of Guelph, Ontario, Canada, one of the members of the Syngenta-sponsored team, found that lower levels of atrazine did not induce aromatase, a result that, if true, would undermine Hayes's speculation. With an aromatase link, "there should be a correlation between dose and response," Solomon said. "But the highest proportion of abnormalities was found at a site with atrazine levels close to background. On this basis how can the cause be atrazine?" As for the lab-based findings, he wrote: "If this effect is robust, [our] new laboratory study on *Xenopus* [African clawed frog] should produce clear results—it doesn't."[23] The controversy, which persists today, was now fully engaged.

The theory cited by Hayes and other atrazine ban proponents—that the herbicide is an "endocrine disruptor" whose effects show up most noticeably when animals are exposed to low doses—is known as the "new paradigm." The zoologist Theo Colborn has been its most ardent popularizer. While examining fish in the Great Lakes during the 1980s, Colborn had found evidence that some chemicals impacted brain development in newborns. The findings were concerning and warranted serious follow-up to evaluate the potential impact of these chemicals on humans. She convened a conference of like-minded scientists and activists in Wingspread, Wisconsin, in 1991 to discuss her findings. The Wingspread activists coined the term "endocrine disruptor" to describe any chemical that could have any effect at any dose on the endocrine system of any animal. They promoted their thesis in a sensational, best-selling book, *Our Stolen Future: Are We Threatening Our Fertility, Intelligence and Survival?—A Scientific Detective Story.*[24]

The phrase "endocrine disruption" was clearly designed to be a slogan, not a scientific term or description to be used in an enlightened evaluation of risk. It was not unlike some people calling the estate tax a "death tax" or activists on abortion issues branding themselves "pro-choice" or "pro-life." At first, journalists and other scientists put the term in quotation marks to signify that this was a highly charged political term, but over time the quotation marks disappeared. The term soon emerged as a rallying cry for activists arguing for restrictions on a range of once innocuous but now controversial chemicals, such as atrazine and bisphenol A.

Although the term "endocrine disruption" is now widely used in the media and by some scientists, many other scientists believe it is used misleadingly. Many natural substances, including clover, many fruits, and soy—together called phytoestrogens—subtly alter the way our hormones work. They are what scientists call "endocrine mediators," a far less incendiary and politicized term than "endocrine disruptor" that has largely fallen out of use. It has been shown that triazines (including atrazine), among a variety of synthetic chemicals, can also act as subtle mediators, impacting our endocrine system. However, the majority of scientists remain convinced that because the typical level of exposure is so low, neither phytoestrogens nor many estrogenic chemicals, including atrazine, pose a danger to human health.

The world is awash in chemicals, natural and human-made. Approximately one hundred thousand synthetic chemicals are approved for consumer products and industrial processes, and very few are considered harmful at levels detected in humans. Whereas precautionary thinking is easy to grasp and plays into our instinctual fear of the unknown, the concept of relative risk is very hard for most nonscientists, including many journalists, to get their minds around.

Rebranding the normal range of effects that certain chemicals have on the human endocrine system as an "endocrine disruptor" is about as useful as describing a car as "fast." Terms such as "neurotoxic" or "endocrine disruptor" sound alarming, but they say nothing about how much of a substance might be problematic. Relative to what? Under what conditions? The question for regulators remains: how much of a substance causes a deleterious effect? As Paracelsus, the father of toxicology, observed, "All things are poison and nothing is without poison; only the dose permits something not to be poisonous." Many natural substances in our foods are toxic, including some essential and beneficial vitamins and minerals, when consumed in large enough quantities. To put this in perspective, vitamin D—an essential vitamin for life—has about the same toxicity as arsenic. Knowing the effect and the dose at which that effect can occur is the evidence-based process used by the EPA to regulate chemicals. The precautionary principle, on the other hand, asks only for effect and then demands action without the context of exposure. The only significant science-based question is whether a particular substance is harmful at the trace level at which it is metabolized in the human body.

Without context, "endocrine disruptor" is an emotionally charged phrase with questionable useful application. Because hormones operate at extremely low concentrations, even tiny doses of an endocrine mediator can have an effect. But most scientists and regulators remain dubious that low doses of certain chemicals, natural or synthetic, significantly disrupt the human metabolic and reproductive systems. Many natural or synthetic chemicals labeled endocrine disruptors are millions of times less potent than estrogen or testosterone and simply do not have the "punch" to overwhelm the endocrine system. For atrazine, the discerning factor is potency relative to estrogen or testosterone. Studies that apply classic risk analysis have consistently shown that "a risk to human health [from atrazine is] essentially nonexistent."[25]

The Politics of Atrazine Research

The case against atrazine rests largely on the integrity of the central body of research by its chief critic, Professor Hayes. For example, a widely circulated joint polemic issued in January 2010 by the Land Stewardship Project and PAN cites Hayes more than fifty times and includes a question-and-answer section with him in which he outlines his allegations.[26] However, many government regulators and independent scientists have raised serious questions about the reliability of his data. "Atrazine has been used widely in South Africa for the past 45 years, and our studies showed that *Xenopus* are doing equally fine in agricultural and nonagricultural areas," reported zoologist Louis du Preez of North-West University in South Africa in one recent commentary on Hayes's work. African clawed frogs do not appear to be suffering from the herbicide in their native habitats reported in response. "If atrazine had these adverse effects on *Xenopus* in the wild, surely we would have picked it up by now."[27]

The EPA and the government's independent SAP have doggedly tried to replicate Hayes's findings, but to no avail. In 2005, the agency published a ninety-five-page white paper, concluding that Hayes's work and other studies on atrazine were "scientifically flawed." Anne Lindsay, then the deputy director of the Office of Pesticide Programs, testified that the EPA "has never seen either the results from any independent investigator published in peer-reviewed scientific journals or the raw data from Hayes' additional experiments that confirm Dr. Hayes' conclusions." According to Lindsay, "The existing data are insufficient to demonstrate that atrazine causes such effects [aromatase induction]."[28]

The controversy did not fade, however, as advocacy groups continued to cite Hayes's findings and to press regulators to ban atrazine. Facing intense public scrutiny stirred by the media, the EPA required Syngenta to fund extensive additional independent studies, which were carried out in two separate independent labs in the United States and Germany—the most extensive reviews ever undertaken on atrazine. Both studies refuted Hayes's conclusions. Biologist Werner Kloas of Humboldt University in Berlin found no impact on clawed frogs at concentrations comparable to those investigated by Hayes. He suspected that Hayes's samples might have mixed with traces of bisphenol A, a chemical additive that is known to leach from plastic containers (the frogs lived in them) or that problems might have been introduced during screening. He also questioned the single exposure level used by Hayes in his study and the lack of measurement of female hormone levels in the affected frogs. Kloas's findings are particularly noteworthy because he has publicly expressed his view that a chemical should be banned for precautionary reasons if there is documented proof, however incomplete, questioning its safety.[29]

After an SAP review of all the data, in 2007 the EPA concluded, "There is no compelling reason to pursue additional testing."[30] But that definitive assessment did not deter critics. Although the two Syngenta-funded studies were conducted under the strictest application of EPA's "Good Laboratory Practice Standards" and were thoroughly audited and inspected, data point by data point, by the EPA, advocacy groups dismissed them and all studies in which the industry participated or funded as automatically tainted because of the industry links.

That sweeping denunciation demonstrates a fundamental lack of understanding of the process of evaluating and approving chemicals. Chemical companies do not fund safety studies as public relations exercises; they fund them because the law requires them to do so. In the case of atrazine, the Federal Insecticide, Fungicide, and Rodenticide Act (FIFRA) places the burden of proving safety on pesticide companies. For a chemical such as atrazine to be approved, it must undergo a battery of tests designed by the EPA and often carried out by independent, third-party laboratories. All data must adhere to rigorous, internationally recognized Quality Assurance Protocols, and documentation can run to hundreds of pages. The process is transparent. All the raw data are available to EPA auditors, who often sit down with the scientists to examine the conclusions, point by point. If the EPA determines that a test is not sufficient, it requires companies to fund and perform additional tests.

In contrast, the peer review process is not very efficient in sorting out quality research from bad peer-reviewed papers. Journal articles do not require editorial oversight or government audits. A manuscript often contains only a few paragraphs explaining the methodology behind the study and little information, if any, about quality assurance procedures. Reviewers rarely have access to the raw data summarized in the paper, and study authors decide for themselves whether to respond to reviewer comments and questions, let alone engage in dialogue with them.

Hayes's work has been peer reviewed for journal articles, but the data remain in a proverbial black box to regulators and other scientists. Because of the storm of controversy fanned by the NRDC and other advocacy groups, in 2008 the Australian government's Department of Environment, Water, Heritage and the Arts reviewed all of Hayes's studies to that point. Its conclusion: "Atrazine is unlikely to have an adverse impact on frogs at existing levels of exposure."[31] That same year, in experiments that closely replicated Hayes's study outline, endocrinologist Taisen Iguchi at the Okazaki Institute for Integrative Bioscience (Japan) and colleagues raised tadpoles in various concentrations of atrazine and found no hermaphroditic frogs.[32] After reviewing the data, endocrinologist Robert Denver of the University of Michigan, well recognized for his independence, commented that the experiments "appear to be carefully executed and the data thoughtfully interpreted. Overall, this appears to be a sound study that does not support the view that atrazine adversely affects amphibian gonadal development through an estrogenic action."[33]

Also in 2008, Keith Solomon, by then head of the Centre for Toxicology at the University of Guelph, reviewed more than 130 recent studies on atrazine for *Critical Reviews in Toxicology*, a well-regarded international journal. The team's conclusion: Most studies found atrazine had no significant effects, and even in cases where effects were found, they were not substantial enough to warrant concern:

> We have brought the results and conclusions of all of the relevant laboratory and field studies together in this critical review....Based on a weight of evidence analysis of all of the data, the central theory that environmentally relevant concentrations of atrazine affect reproduction and/or reproductive development in fish, amphibians, and reptiles is not supported by the vast majority of observations. The same conclusions also hold for the supporting theories such as induction of aromatase, the enzyme that converts testosterone to estradiol. For other responses, such as immune function, stress endocrinology, parasitism, or population-level effects, there are no indications of effects or there is such a paucity of good data that definitive conclusions cannot be made.[34]

Although a massive meta-analysis published in fall 2009 raised some concerns about the effects of atrazine, it pointedly noted that Hayes and only Hayes has found that atrazine increased aromatase and that no study has found it affects vitellogenin, a protein that should be expressed if atrazine was seriously impacting the endocrine system. Its conclusion: "These data do not support the hypothesis that atrazine is strongly estrogenic to fish."[35] If that conclusion is accurate, much of the case damning atrazine as a potentially harmful endocrine disruptor collapses.

Most recently, in March 2010, Hayes was the lead author on a paper published by the National Academy of Sciences arguing that atrazine demasculinized frogs throughout all life stages, from tadpole to adult, when they were exposed to a single dose below 3 ppb, which, as noted earlier, is below the protective outer limit considered acceptable by the EPA for humans (but it must be noted, as it includes a safety factor in the thousands, it is not a level at which any actual harm has been found in humans). The problem, Hayes and his team speculated, was that atrazine absorbed through the frogs' skin turns on a gene that in male frogs should stay off, which converts testosterone into estrogen, flooding the frog's body with the wrong chemical signal.[36] Although the study sounds alarming, no other research team, independent or industry funded, has found similar effects (again, at levels a thousand times or more higher than has impacted any animal). Australia's Department of Environment, Water, Heritage and the Arts reviewed the new study, found it wanting, and said there was not sufficient evidence to reconsider its current conclusion that atrazine is safe as currently used.[37]

The EPA has been eager to review the data from Hayes' various studies, but the Berkeley professor has steadfastly refused to cooperate with regulators. After years of frustration, in a May 2010 letter, the agency's Donald Brady, director of the EPA's Environmental Fate and Effects Division, Office of Pesticide Programs, issued a highly unusual rebuke of a scientist in a response to an inquiry from Illinois state representative Dave Winters, who had contacted the EPA after Hayes testified before the state legislature urging a ban on the pesticide:

> As with most reviews conducted by the EPA, the analysis of data and studies is not limited to a single individual [at EPA] but rather involves interdisciplinary scientific teams and multiple rounds of peer review. You [Winter] asked whether EPA was in agreement with Dr. Hayes' findings.... I regret that the EPA science staff in the Office of Pesticide Programs' EFED could not properly account for the sample sizes and study design reportedly used by the Berkeley researchers. As a result, we were unable to complete any independent analysis to support the study's conclusions.[38]

One would think that the uniform rejections of Hayes's studies by internationally respected toxicology laboratories and regulatory agencies would make headlines at least comparable to the scare stories that regularly have appeared after the publication of each of his controversial papers—but they didn't.

Why have journalists not provided a balanced perspective on atrazine in particular and chemicals in general? Simply stated, many reporters are poorly schooled in science. They often do not have the sophistication or inclination to apply "weight of evidence" criteria or to critically parse science from ideology. Although new claims that one product or another contains harmful chemicals often result in a sensational front-page story, because of the journalist's default mindset, a study that shows a chemical is safe or has few effects is often ignored or relegated to the back pages. What is the news value in the headline "Atrazine Found Safe; Scientists Conclude Fears Overblown"?

Scientists know about this phenomenon because it also impacts which studies are published. It is called the "file-drawer effect"—the disturbing reality that researchers tend to place the results of experiments that show no or few effects in their file drawer, anticipating that journals are biased against publishing studies showing little or no effects. The media have their own version of this phenomenon: reporting the scare based on scanty data while ignoring the eventual finding of "no serious effects." It is likely that over the years dozens if not hundreds of studies that have found little or no effects from atrazine have been buried or received scant attention—which makes an even stronger case that this critically important agricultural chemical is safe when used appropriately.

A Precautionary Future?

In sum, the scientific evidence to date strongly suggests that atrazine, as it may occur in the environment, does not present a serious danger to aquatic wildlife, let alone to humans. Unable to make headway on the science, atrazine opponents have turned to politics. Farmers face ongoing activist campaigns intended to pressure U.S. regulators into adopting more precautionary policies. Ban proponents have found allies among some legislators. The EPA's announcement in fall 2009 that it would again reevaluate (for the second time in two years) the research on atrazine followed a private September meeting between the EPA's senior staff and the Senate Environmental and Public Works Committee, led by California's Democratic senator Barbara Boxer.[39]

The next EPA review of atrazine promises to be a dramatic test case about whether European hazard standards will be extended to the United States—without congressional review. If the EPA imports and implements this precautionary model, atrazine and other chemicals found safe by classic "weight of evidence" risk assessment studies long used in the

United States would be subject to what would amount to a political review of their acceptability. Such a seismic shift in regulatory standards could lead to restrictions based on suspicions and fears rather than scientific evidence. Trade-offs, such as the higher food costs and the damage to America's farming economy and international competitiveness that a ban would inflict, could be downplayed or ignored.

Norman Borlaug, the father of the Green Revolution in the latter half of the twentieth century, said a few years before his death in 2009 that if the new plant varieties he created "had been subjected to the kinds of regulatory strictures and requirements that are being inflicted today, they would never have become available."[40] This, of course, is the ultimate trade-off that ban proponents have yet to face up to—what removing essential tools such as atrazine would mean for the world's ability to feed an expanding population. It is generally acknowledged that by 2050, we will have to grow twice as much as we do today, and on the same amount of land we now use, unless we want to denude our planet of forests. Organic farming, which produces some 40 percent less than modern farming techniques, is not an option. If the precautionary view prevails, the unintended consequences could include more soil erosion, less sustainable farming, more environmental degradation—and a hungrier world.

Notes

1. According to the Department of Energy, "Researchers estimate that the extensive adoption of no-till agriculture, diversified rotations, cover crops, fertility management, erosion control and irrigation management can lead to the recovery of two thirds of the carbon that has been lost from the soil due to conversion of native ecosystems to agriculture and the use of conventional management practices." Also see "Less Is More: No-Till Agriculture Helps Mitigate Global Warming," *U.S. Energy News*, September 2009, http://www.E.U.rekalert.org/features/doe/2005-09/dnnl-lim091605.php.

2. U.S. Environmental Protection Agency, Biological and Economic Analysis Division, "Assessment of Potential Mitigation Measures for Atrazine," 2002, www.btny.purdue.edu/ppp/ABA-02-03.pdf.

3. Richard Fawcett, "Twenty Years of Corn Yield with and without Atrazine, North Central Weed Science Society, 2008, http://www.ncwss.org/proceed/2008/abstracts/137.pdf.

4. F. Ackerman, "The Economics of Atrazine," *International Journal of Occupational and Environmental Health* 13, no. 4 (October/December 2007): 437–45.

5. K. R. Solomon et al., "Ecological Risk Assessment of Atrazine in North American Surface Waters," *Environmental Toxicology and Chemistry* 15 (1996): 31–76.

6 UK Rapporteur Monograph, "Atrazine: Report and Proposed Decision of the United Kingdom Made to the European Commission under Article 7(1) of Regulation 3600/92 Council Directive 91/4 14/EEC Regulation 3600/92," United Kingdom Pesticide Directorate, October 1996.

7. "Opinion of the Scientific Committee on Plants on Specific Questions from the Commission concerning the Evaluation of Atrazine in the Context of Council Directive 91/414/EEC" (Brussels: Health and Consumer Protection Directorate-General, Scientific Committee on Plants, European Commission, SCP/ATRAZINE/002-Final, 2003).

8. "Re-evaluation Decision Document: Atrazine," *Health Canada*, May 25, 2004, http://www.hc-sc.gc.ca/cps-spc/pubs/pest/_decisions/rrd2004-12/index-eng.php.

9. "Atrazine," *International Agency for Research on Cancer Monographs* 73 (1999): 59–113, http://monographs.iarc.fr/ENG/Monographs/vol73/mono73-8.pdf.

10. Australian Pesticides and Veterinary Medicines Authority, "Chemicals in the News: Atrazine," March 19, 2010, http://202.125.15.27/news_media/chemicals/atrazine.php.

11. Ibid., "Chemicals in the News: Atrazine," May 31, 2010, http://www.apvma.gov.au/news_media/chemicals/atrazine.php#amphibians.

12. Natural Resources Defense Council, "Atrazine: Poisoning the Well: How the EPA Is Ignoring Atrazine Contamination in the Central United States," August 22, 2009, http://www.nrdc.org/health/atrazine/default.asp.

13. "EPA Begins New Scientific Evaluation of Atrazine," EPA News Release, October 7, 2009, http://yosemite.epa.gov/opa/admpress.nsf/8b770facf5edf6f185257359003fb69e/554b6abea9d0672f85257648004a88c1!OpenDocumnt.

14. "DEP Study Shows No Risk from Pharmaceuticals and Personal Care Products in NYC Drinking Water," May 27, 2010, http://www.nyc.gov/html/dep/html/press_releases/10-55pr.shtml.

15. Michael Howard Saul, "City's Water Tests Clean," Wall Street Journal, May 27, 2010, http://online.wsj.com/article/SB10001424052748704032704575726898342 1433118.html?mod=googlenews_wsj.

16. World Health Organization, Water Sanitation and Health (WSH), "Chemical Hazards in Drinking-Water—Atrazine," Background and Summary Statements for the Fourth Edition, October 1, 2010, http://www.who.int/water_sanitation_health/dwq/chemicals/atrazine/en/.

17. R. J. Gilliam et al., "The Quality of Our Nation's Waters: Pesticides in the Nation's Streams and Ground Water, 1992–2001," U.S. Geological Survey Circular 1291 (2006).

18. D. J. Sullivan et al., "Trends in Pesticide Concentrations in Corn-Belt Streams, 1996–2006," USGS Scientific Investigations Report 2009-5132, http://pubs.usgs.gov/sir/2009/5132.

19. Natural Resources Defense Council, "Atrazine: Poisoning the Well."

20. William Souder, "As EPA Re-Evaluates Safety of Herbicide Atrazine, Minnesota Conducts Its Own Review," MinnPost.com, October 28, 2009, www.minnpost.com/stories/2009/10/28/12903/as_epa_re-evaluates_safety_of_herbicide_atrazine_minnesota_conducts_its_own_review.

21. "Triazine Cumulative Risk Assessment," USEPA Office of Pesticide Programs, Health Effects Division, March 28, 2006.

22. T. B. Hayes et al., "Hermaphroditic, Demasculinized Frogs after Exposure to the Herbicide Atrazine at Low Ecologically Relevant Doses," PNAS 99, no. 8 (April 16, 2002): 5476–80.

23. Rebecca Renner, "Controversy Lingers over Herbicides' Link to Frog Deformities," Science, November 1, 2002, 938–39.

24. T. Colborn et al., Our Stolen Future: Are We Threatening Our Fertility, Intelligence and Survival?—A Scientific Detective Story (New York: Penguin Books, 1996).

25. For one of numerous studies, see R. L. Cooper et al., "Effect of Atrazine on Ovarian Function in the Rat," *Reproductive Toxicology* 13, no. 6 (1996): 491–99.

26. Land Stewardship Project and Pesticide Action Network, "The Syngenta Corporation and Atrazine: The Cost to the Land, People and Democracy," January 2010, 1, www.landstewardshipproject.org/pdf/AtrazineReportJan2010.pdf.

27. David Biello, "Sex-Changing Weed Killer," *Scientific American*, May 2010, http://www.scientificamerican.com/article.cfm?id=sex-changing-weed-killer.

28. Statement of EPA's Anne E. Lindsay, Minnesota House of Representatives, February 16, 2005, www.atrazine.com/atrazine/images/Lindsay_written.pdf.

29. Biello, "Sex-Changing Weed Killer."

30. U.S. Environmental Protection Agency, "Pesticide News Story: Scientific Advisory Panel to Discuss Amphibian Gonadal Development; White Paper Posted to Docket," September 24, 2007, http://www.epa.gov/oppfead1/cb/csb_page/updates/2007/sap-mtg-atrazine.htm.

31. Australian Pesticides and Veterinary Medicines Authority, "Chemicals in the News: Atrazine."

32. T. Oka et al., "Effect of Atrazine on Metamorphosis and Sexual Differentiation in *Xenopus Laevis*," *Aquatic Toxicology* 7, no. 4 (2008): 215–26.

33. Rebecca Renner, "Atrazine Effects in Xenopus Aren't Reproducible," *Environmental Science and Technology*, May 15, 2008, 3491–93.

34. Keith Solomon, "Effects of Atrazine on Fish, Amphibians, and Aquatic Reptiles: A Critical Review," *Critical Reviews in Toxicology* 38, no. 9 (2008): 721–72.

35. J. R. Rohr and K. A. McCoy, "A Qualitative Meta-Analysis Reveals Consistent Effects of Atrazine on Freshwater Fish and Amphibians," *Environmental Health Perspectives* 118, no. 1 (January 2010): 20–32.

36. T. B. Hayes et al., "Atrazine Induces Complete Feminization and Chemical Castration in Male African Clawed Frogs (*Xenopus Laevis*), March 1, 2010, http://www.pnas.org/content/early/2010/02/12/0909519107.abstract.

37. Australian Pesticides and Veterinary Medicines Authority, "Chemicals in the News: Atrazine."

38. Letter from U.S. EPA's Donald Brady to Illinois State Representative Dave Winters, May 17, 2010, http://agsense.org/epa-responds-to-illinois-rep-concerning-hayes-atrazine-based-frog-gonad-assertions/.

39. Danielle Ivory, "In Reversal of Bush Policy, EPA Launches New Study of Atrazine's Health Effects," *Huffington Post*, October 7, 2009, http://www.huffingtonpost.com/tag/epa-atrazine.

40. Norman Borlaug, "Foreword," in *The Frankenfood Myth: How Protest and Politics Threaten the Biotech Revolution*, by Henry Miller and Greg Conko (Praeger Publishers, 2004), available at: http://www.agbioworld.org/biotech-info/topics/borlaug/frankenfood-myth.html.

4

The Tart Cherry:
Pesticides and Precaution

Mark Whalon and Jeanette Wilson

Pesticides, including bactericides, fungicides, herbicides, insecticides, nematicides, and rodenticides, have many uses and, in some cases, far-reaching market, economic, ecological, and environmental impacts. Pesticide manufacturers and grower groups frequently argue that as agricultural tools, pesticides ensure and increase both the quality and the quantity of the U.S. food supply and that their use complies with sound food safety, conforms to environmental wholesomeness, and meets the critical food security needs of the United States. Most growers, handlers, processors, haulers, workers, and marketers recognize the essential role that these pesticides contribute to an abundant, healthy, and reliable food system in the United States. Without new and paradigm-shifting technologies, pesticides will remain essential; indeed, their demise would undoubtedly bring about a return to the destruction and waste of agricultural production typical of previous centuries. The vast infrastructure of society's fresh produce, stored products, and packaged foods would be contaminated or putrefied, and most grains, fresh fruits, and vegetables could not be produced on the scale needed to maintain U.S. citizens' health and welfare. This infrastructure, predicated on pesticides, represents a complex reality undergirding U.S. society through agricultural, transportation, and numerous market, delivery, and consumption processes. This in no way denigrates or puts aside organic production, which in the specialty crop arena is just as reliant on "pesticides" to effectively produce a marketable crop. Very little produce available to consumers today has not been treated with pesticides.

We recognize that a "one size fits all" mentality sees pesticides as environmental poisons and a cause of undue human health risks. This view may have merit in some instances, but not in most cases. Although it is desirable to work toward replacing hazardous pesticide use with ecologically sound and socially just alternatives, this process should not focus only on the elimination of pesticides with poor reputations or those with a history of faulty use as though this history is the sole fault of the chemistry itself. Chemistry cannot adjust for non-label use, bad decisions, egregious human behavior, or disregard for the law or the land. Yet society cannot afford the consequences of ignoring the food security, health, and green benefits that may be lost if a "one size fits all" or precautionary approach to pesticide policy is adopted, particularly one that ignores the good that some otherwise dangerous pesticides may have if used correctly. In this chapter, after providing a brief history of U.S. pesticide legislation, we explore how a seemingly human-health-friendly piece of legislation, the Food Quality Protection Act (FQPA), could actually result in higher pesticide residues in fresh and processed products. Then, using the example of a specialty crop, the tart cherry, we will see how this legislation contributed to greater disruption of this particular crop's production ecosystems, and perhaps now is leading to economic collapse of a once healthy industry. We will also discuss how this legislation serves as an example for not adopting certain broad-sweeping regulatory generalizations, like the precautionary principle, and, finally, look at future implications of current policies.

A Brief History of U.S. Pesticide Legislation

Pesticide legislation in the United States was initially enacted in the early 1900s to protect farmers from the fraudulent claims of hucksters.[1] Since then, pesticide regulatory efforts have expanded and diversified in purpose, with the intent of protecting humans, animals, and the environment. Unfortunately, policy efforts have too often led to a society-directed "command and control" approach to pesticide use rather than facilitating the adoption of new Integrated Pest Management practices by growers.[2] U.S.

pesticide legislation (figure 4-1) has traditionally been aimed at ensuring environmental, producer, worker, and handler safety, more recently also moving to ensure ecological health. Two relatively early pieces of legislation that set the stage for this "command and control" approach were the Federal Food, Drug, and Cosmetic Act (FFDCA) of 1938 and the Federal Insecticide, Fungicide, and Rodenticide Act (FIFRA) of 1947.[3] The FFDCA limits pesticide residues on food and animal feed, and the FIFRA is a product-licensing statute that governs the manufacture, handling, sale, and use of pesticide products in the United States.

FIGURE 4-1

SUMMARY OF U.S. PESTICIDE LEGISLATION FROM 1900 TO THE PRESENT

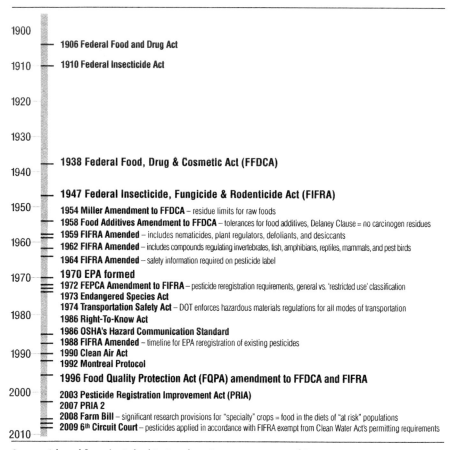

1900	
1910	1906 Federal Food and Drug Act
	1910 Federal Insecticide Act
1920	
1930	
1940	1938 Federal Food, Drug & Cosmetic Act (FFDCA)
1950	1947 Federal Insecticide, Fungicide & Rodenticide Act (FIFRA)
	1954 Miller Amendment to FFDCA – residue limits for raw foods
	1958 Food Additives Amendment to FFDCA – tolerances for food additives, Delaney Clause = no carcinogen residues
1960	1959 FIFRA Amended – includes nematicides, plant regulators, defoliants, and desiccants
	1962 FIFRA Amended – includes compounds regulating invertebrates, fish, amphibians, reptiles, mammals, and pest birds
	1964 FIFRA Amended – safety information required on pesticide label
1970	1970 EPA formed
	1972 FEPCA Amendment to FIFRA – pesticide reregistration requirements, general vs. 'restricted use' classification
	1973 Endangered Species Act
1980	1974 Transportation Safety Act – DOT enforces hazardous materials regulations for all modes of transportation
	1986 Right-To-Know Act
	1986 OSHA's Hazard Communication Standard
	1988 FIFRA Amended – timeline for EPA reregistration of existing pesticides
1990	1990 Clean Air Act
	1992 Montreal Protocol
	1996 Food Quality Protection Act (FQPA) amendment to FFDCA and FIFRA
2000	2003 Pesticide Registration Improvement Act (PRIA)
	2007 PRIA 2
	2008 Farm Bill – significant research provisions for "specialty" crops = food in the diets of "at risk" populations
2010	2009 6th Circuit Court – pesticides applied in accordance with FIFRA exempt from Clean Water Act's permitting requirements

SOURCE: Adapted from the Federal Register, http://www.gpoaccess.gov/fr/.

Both pieces of legislation have been updated and amended numerous times since their inception.[4] A 1958 amendment to the prior FFDCA legislation targeted pesticide residues in terms of their total risk. A subsequent amendment introduced the Delaney Clause, which mandated that tolerance levels be set for the regulation of carcinogens in processed food, but not fresh food. The original 1947 FIFRA required that all pesticides be registered by the U.S. Department of Agriculture (USDA) to be eligible for commercial use. In 1964 an amendment authorized the secretary of agriculture to refuse pesticide registration to products that were deemed "unsafe or ineffective." Pesticide registration and administration of the FIFRA was transferred to the Environmental Protection Agency on its creation in 1970. This dramatically shifted the focus of federal pesticide regulation from controlling pesticides for safe use in agricultural production, which was an agricultural production facilitation role, to one of "command and control" of agricultural use of pesticides in the environment.

Regulatory Changes under the Food Quality Protection Act

The passage of the Food Quality Protection Act in 1996 significantly altered the pesticide regulation landscape. The FQPA amended both the FIFRA and the FFDCA in an attempt to resolve inconsistencies in these two statutes. The FQPA raised the standard of worker and applicator pesticide exposure protection and greatly altered and expanded the manner in which the EPA performed risk assessments. Because the FQPA resolved and unified the regulation disparity between processed and nonprocessed foods, it solved the Delaney paradox. Yet, in stark contrast to the rather myopic Delaney issue, the FQPA reworked much of the United States' pesticide regulatory apparatus by amending the "risk cup," looking at the risk associated with exposure to the cumulative residues for all compounds exhibiting the same binding site. For the first time it treated pesticides on food as contaminants whose level must be approved by the agency according to the cumulative risk of the toxicant. Other key changes gave definitive structure and more specific use of incident reporting, worker exposure, measurable or inferred environmental impacts, endocrine disruption risks, use of ecological assessment data, pollinator protection, and even pesticide resistance management.[5]

The FQPA's new mantra became "reasonable certainty of no harm" and with it were formed an array of new safety standards, especially for pesticides used on food crops, and a logical process whereby the EPA would resolve public comment, input, and participation in pesticide decisions, particularly for reregistrations (figure 4-2). Yet these were by no means the only major changes the FQPA brought forward. The laws passed after the FQPA, such as the Pesticide Registration Improvement Act, created a major reregistration framework.[6] The FQPA also ushered in a new era in pesticide classification by introducing such terms as "reduced risk" and "organophosphate alternative" classifications of pesticides. More discussion of these classifications and their subsequent outcome on tart cherries in the Upper Midwest follows.

Overall, the EPA's adaptive processes reflected good government. When the FQPA was passed, EPA staff put forth an effort to engage relevant stakeholders and the public in establishing a protocol for implementing the changes to the pesticide reregistration process under the law. The EPA's Pesticide Programs Dialogue Committee, Tolerance Reassessment Advisory Committee, Committee to Advise on Reassessment and Transition, and other USDA federal advisory boards were established to provide the agency with advice on strategic approaches to transition under the FQPA. From these processes, the agency developed a logical and publically vetted six-phase tolerance reassessment and reregistration public participation process that is now routinely employed by the agency. These practices were put in place after open public interaction with all stakeholders, including pesticide registrants, the USDA, environmental organizations, physicians, scientists, and other government agencies (for example, the Food and Drug Administration) as appropriate.

The Impact of the Food Quality Protection Act on the Tart Cherry Industry

The main issues that arose from the FQPA for tart cherry producers were those brought on by the "one size fits all" pesticide phaseouts, with little

FIGURE 4-2

**EPA PESTICIDE REREGISTRATION PROCESS IMPLEMENTED
UNDER THE FOOD QUALITY PROTECTION ACT**

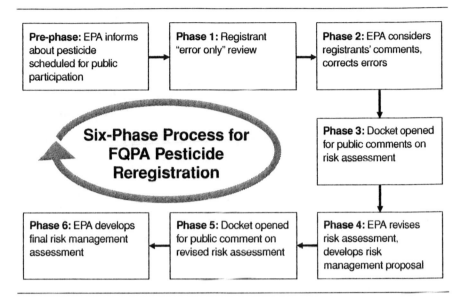

SOURCE: Adapted from the Environmental Protection Agency, http://www.epa.gov/oppsrrd1/reregistration/
public_summaries.htm#6phase.

regard for whether the outcome would be economically devastating, more environmentally impacting, or more ecologically disruptive and/or whether the outcome would add five new toxicant modes of action to the pest management system in less than five years. For example, the removal from the market of the agricultural chemical azinphosmethyl (AZM), an organophosphate widely used on processed tart cherries, was carried forward with little scientifically justified data regarding worker exposure, fruit residue, or insecticide drift from actual tart cherry production. The legislation has forced tart cherry producers to introduce numerous new compounds that actually put more residues on the cherries for the consumer and that in turn have brought on problems with maximum residue levels in some of the industry's most important overseas markets.[7] Although the FQPA resolved a number of problems in U.S. pesticide registration and reregistration, it failed to develop a means of addressing a science- and ecology-based assessment of current and future pesticides. In some systems, such as tart cherries, it has led to less sustainable agriculture, which greatly endangers the viability of small- to medium-size family farms in the Upper Midwest. We have summarized the overall effects of the FQPA on tart cherries in table 4-1.

TABLE 4-1
TART CHERRY INDUSTRY'S VIEW OF THE
IMPACTS OF THE FOOD QUALITY PROTECTION ACT

Pre-FQPA	Post-FQPA
Refined Integrated Pest Management System	Fall Back to a Calendar Spray
Fairly Simple Pest Management	Increased Complexity
Solid Efficacy = Low Risk	Risk of Crop Failure
Stable Ecosystems	Increased Ecological Impacts
Known Environmental Impacts	Unknown Environmental Impacts

SOURCE: Authors' diagram.

The FQPA was supported in Congress as a way to reduce cancer risks, reduce pesticide residues, and thereby reduce risk to humans and the environment. We have conducted comprehensive studies across three states (Michigan, Wisconsin, and Utah), attempting to evaluate the economics, efficacy, residues, and ecological impacts of FQPA changes on tart cherry production.[8] (Approximately 70 percent of U.S. tart cherries are grown, processed, and marketed in Michigan; Utah has about 8 percent of production; and Wisconsin has about 3 percent of production.[9]) In these studies, we monitored the effects of the FQPA and AZM-based pest management systems on beneficial species in replicated tart cherry orchards from southwest to northwest Michigan. The studies were large-block (eight to twenty acres), side-by-side tart cherry orchards treated with either AZM (historically valid standard practices pre-FQPA) or the FQPA-induced best-practice systems available today. Ecological impacts were judged by the perturbation of thirty-two beneficial arthropod taxa typically found in tart cherry orchards.[10] These data were compiled across eighteen paired

FIGURE 4-3

ECOLOGICAL IMPACTS OF ORGANOPHOSPHATE-BASED VERSUS FOOD QUALITY PROTECTION ACT INSECTICIDE PROGRAMS ON ORCHARD ECOLOGY

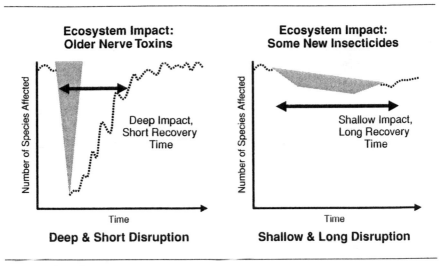

FQPA- versus AZM-based orchards. Figure 4-3 summarizes the characterization of both systems' ecological impacts. We also calculated the economic returns to the grower for biological control resulting from the presence of natural beneficial species. The AZM-based orchards yielded a higher economic return per acre for biological control. These studies reveal a picture of the ecological "health" of tart cherry orchards before and after FQPA

To indict AZM ecologically, the EPA initially cited instances where AZM aerial application on Florida sugarcane and Arkansas rice produced fish kills as examples of what AZM was doing in the Upper Midwest. These aquaculture AZM incidents were severe, and the evidence seemed damning, but these data were irrelevant for tart cherries in the Upper Midwest. Michigan cherries are not sprayed from the air, and cherries are not grown in water. The industry's response to these incident reports stated that Michigan has never had a reported AZM water incident from tart cherry orchard spraying even though most Michigan orchards reside within a mile of running water, active streams, ponds, or lakes. If AZM was impacting aquatic ecosystems as drastically as implied by these incident risk assessment reports, hundreds or perhaps thousands of fish kills would have been reported. This issue is very significant because these documented incidents should have elicited agency action in sugarcane and rice, but not in tart cherry orchards. These incidents cast a dark shadow over AZM's use, even though no such incidents had ever been recorded in more than forty years of AZM use in Michigan. Moreover, the mechanical method of harvesting tart cherries directly into water bins yields little or no worker exposure, and AZM residues on the fruit have so weathered by harvest time that the tart cherry production system has never had any AZM incidents where a measurement of maximum residue levels led to the cancellation of entry in any global market. Furthermore, in a concerted effort to document actual residues in tart cherry production, a study commissioned by the Michigan Department of Agriculture, in conjunction with Michigan State University, secured replicated data from both harvested cherries and bin water at harvest and submitted these data to the EPA. These data showed that it was difficult to detect AZM residues on the fruit at harvest and that AZM residues in the harvest water were diminishingly small.[11]

The EPA's lack of knowledge regarding tart cherry production and its irrelevant use of ecological incidents primed the AZM reregistration process to provide less effective insecticide replacements in tart cherries. In addition, in our study of the Michigan Department of Agriculture's records from the early 1960s to date, we did not find a reported case of human poisoning from tart cherry growers' use of AZM. Thus, with no human acute toxicity issue, virtually zero residues at harvest, and no ecological incident report in more than forty years, the EPA's "one size fits all" reregistration processes had little merit where tart cherry AZM use was concerned. Yet today, tart cherry producers have been forced to live with the economic, environmental, ecological, and increased residue repercussions resulting from the aftermath of the FQPA's implementation process for this commodity.

We also note that the passage of the FQPA has led to increases in the cost of specialty crop production[12] and has significantly impacted ecological sustainability in tart cherries as well as other specialty crop systems across North America.[13] Ultimately, the passage of the FQPA may account for the demise of this once-vital industry for hundreds of Upper Midwest communities and thousands of families. Much new information is available

FIGURE 4-4

TREND OF AVERAGE INSECTICIDE COSTS PER ACRE FROM 2004 TO 2009 BETWEEN REDUCED-RISK AND CONVENTIONAL PEST MANAGEMENT SYSTEMS IN NINE MICHIGAN TART CHERRY ORCHARDS

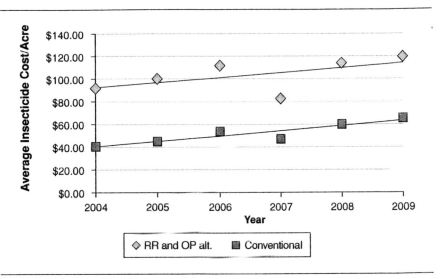

SOURCE: Adapted from Whalon lab research under the Risk Avoidance and Mitigation Program.

NOTES: RR and OP alt. = reduced risk and organophosphate alternative compounds, Conventional = conventional pesticides, including AZM and other organophosphates. Graph shows data from ten orchards in 2008 and 2009.

to the EPA on the pest challenges, ecological costs, and economic and foreign market impacts associated with canceling AZM in tart cherries, but the tart cherry industry is not anticipating a science-based response. The agency's impact estimates have misrepresented and underestimated the economic impacts that the loss of AZM is actually having on this industry, and, unfortunately, under the FQPA there is no statutory requirement for economic impact assessment and remediation unlike those in FIFRA.[14] This economic underestimation of the actual impacts on the tart cherry industry is egregious, especially after a number of warnings to the agency to this effect during the comment phase of its deliberations.[15] We would submit that our research under the USDA Risk Avoidance Mitigation Program over the past six years (figure 4-4) demonstrates that the actual economic cost of replacing AZM is much higher than that estimated by the

EPA and that the agency ought to consider actual science-based data rather than economic speculation.

Global Long-Term Implications

Looking to current and future impacts of the FQPA on the tart cherry industry and other commodities, we would be remiss not to consider factors beyond the scope of U.S. pesticide legislation. In today's global economy, we argue, it is just as important to realize that other countries will outcompete the U.S. industries where U.S. policy unfairly places its own industries in jeopardy in favor of international industries. This is particularly true for U.S. tart cherries, where the EPA's actions are unscientific and capricious. Why not allow some acreage for tart cherries destined for export to be produced with the use of the more environmentally friendly AZM here in the United States so long as these cherries do not enter the domestic market? This question is facetious because the cherry industry in the United States knows how to grow tart cherries with undetectable residues at harvest. Regulators would not know a domestically produced AZM tart cherry in the marketplace by its residue profile, but they would know an FQPA-produced tart cherry by its profile. Growers could spray a little FQPA-directed insecticide within the preharvest interval just before harvest to put residues in the fruit properly. This scenario, of course, demonstrates the absurdity of the conundrum and the de facto trade barrier with which the FQPA has handcuffed American producers.

Why are we discriminating against our own growers while allowing foreign producers to take previously held international markets? One can only surmise that as the global "green" movement continues, it will strongly affect U.S. regulatory policies in bizarre and sometimes domestically catastrophic ways. With this domestic capriciousness, just who is afraid of the EU's precautionary principle? It likely will not be as variable or economically damaging here in the United States as it is in the EU, unless we are politically and ecologically blind enough to enable our politicians such a destructive tool. In our view, too, the passage of the FQPA actually preempts the precautionary principle. In the following section, we describe how that is so.

Preempting the Precautionary Principle

The European Union's precautionary principle approach sets about introducing nonscientific, policy-based, worldview bias into the regulatory process. We believe that despite its flaws, the EPA's system under the FQPA is a better path to prevent environmental degradation and human health hazards from using a pesticide than the precautionary principle. We would advocate a temporary "usage stop" until the proper science could be implemented.

The passage of the FQPA preempts the precautionary principle by setting a general safety standard of a "reasonable certainty of no harm," which is essentially a rephrasing of "reasonable precaution."[16] Thus, the framers of the FQPA demonstrated precautionary-principle-based preemptive thinking by providing an overprotective approach, as in the cancellation of AZM on U.S. cherries. Ironically, though, the EPA's application of alternative pesticides has resulted in greater ecological and subsequent sociological effects on the regulated industry. Therefore, if one could conclude anything, the FQPA far overreaches its objective of reasonable certainty of no harm from the toxicity of a compound to cause economic, ecological, and sociological harm to the affected tart cherry industry and the communities it serves.

In the United States, the FQPA has provided the EPA with an attempted science-based process with abundant precaution. The FQPA allows the agency to adjust precautionary protection to an additional ten times the safety margin beyond the already existing margin of one hundred times the limit of detection of a pesticide in the diets of infants, children, pregnant women, and the aged and infirm. Also, the FQPA's contribution to pesticide registration policy altered the FIFRA's definition of unreasonable adverse effects where at risk human populations and the environment were considered separately from the risks and benefits of other uses of the same chemistry. We reason that U.S. law already has abundantly cautious provisions to address uncertainty. Existing provisions require the EPA to weigh the risks of public health pesticides against the potential health risks of the pest infestation, resulting disease, or adulteration of the environment by ameliorating the risk through the flexible application of an additional safety margin.

Another provision that preempts the precautionary principle occurs in the FQPA where it instructs the USDA, the EPA, and the Department of Health and Human Services to conduct surveys regarding food consumption, a major route of human pesticide residue exposure. The surveys provide data on U.S. consumption patterns of infants, children, and other vulnerable populations through a massive, national, ongoing collection of information on pesticide residues. Therefore, the FQPA already addresses special dietary protections for these at-risk groups. This legislative activity was based on the recommendations of the National Academy of Sciences report titled *Pesticides in the Diets of Infants and Children.*[17] The FQPA's amendments to the FFDCA deem that any pesticide chemical residue on raw or processed food is unsafe unless a tolerance or exemption is in effect, and they require that the residue is within the limits of the tolerance. Thus, the FQPA followed the spirit of the precautionary principle without the dangers of introducing an increased political bias as a science-preempting tool for political short-term gains. In establishing, modifying, or revoking tolerances and exemptions, the EPA must consider the validity of data from a suite of studies together with the nature of the toxic effects shown, in addition to any available information on human risk and dietary consumption, cumulative effects, aggregate exposure, endocrine disruption, environmental and ecological effects, and other safety factors.

The registration provisions in the FQPA mandated that existing residue tolerances be reviewed within ten years (by 2006) to be sure that they met these regulatory requirements encompassed in the FQPA's science- and health-based safety standards. The FQPA requires the EPA to review pesticide registrations to ensure compliance with the new standards, and it also requires the EPA to expedite the review of "safer" pesticides to get them to market sooner, thereby accelerating the replacement of older and potentially more toxic chemistries. Ecologically speaking, this has not been the case with a number of the organophosphate replacements that went through the EPA, but, in our view, the human safety protections have been overly precautious. The FQPA also mandates periodic registration on a fifteen-year cycle to be sure that up-to-date science is applied, ensuring adequate safety on a routine, reasonable time line. Moreover, if an issue arises, the EPA can invoke a special review at any time. Is this provision not abundantly cautious by any measure? In addition, the law requires the EPA to determine whether practical detection methods exist before establishing a tolerance, thus ensuring less politics and more science in its deliberations. The agency's use of special science and stakeholder science advisory panels have provided regular input from widely varying sectors of society, including political venues, and the EPA hears public views during the period of public comment accommodation in each of its *Federal Register* reports for all its committees.

The Future

Almost all human ecosystems are "disturbed" or disrupted by human activity (figure 4-5). Therefore, why is our domestic pesticide policy taking us back to more perturbed ecosystems when we should be heading to greener pastures? No government agency can actually know what a policy will or will not do ecologically until it is implemented on the land. In any average tart cherry orchard there are more than 690 arthropod species occupying varied niches.[18] A pesticide alters that ecosystem, as does mowing, herbicide use, harvesting, weather, and so forth This complexity is not predictable, nor is it captured legislatively. Agriculture, whether organic, biodynamic, sustainable, conventional, integrated pest management, or other, disrupts ecosystems and biodiversity. With progressive and greener agricultural practices, human impacts may be decreased, presumably leading to more sustainable agroecosystems in the future, but no one really knows what that outcome will be.

Today the impact of legislation, including the FQPA, cannot be assessed from a desk. When solid ecosystem studies have demonstrated that old or new policy has taken agriculture in the wrong direction ecologically, it is logical and prudent to advocate for some reciprocity to revert to former systems or reinvent current systems, or society will not learn to ease its impacts and progress ecologically. Currently, agroecosystems are just too complex to predict policy outcomes before the adoption of those policy changes. The wisest long-term course is to let the data rectify such deficits of policy, as the tart cherry industry has carefully and painstakingly demonstrated to the EPA. With the accelerating pace of new pesticide registrations under the FQPA, much is in store for society to understand, adjust to, and compensate for, because each one of these

FIGURE 4-5

DIVERSITY TRENDS IN DIFFERENT MODES OF AGRICULTURAL PRACTICE,
AS COMPARED TO UNCULTIVATED ECOSYSTEMS

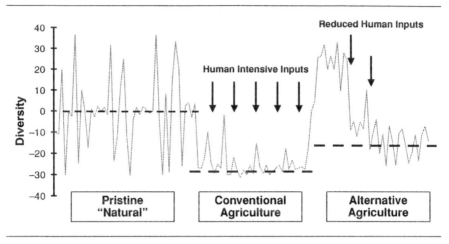

SOURCE: Authors' illustration.

reduced risk and organophosphate-alternative pesticides will disrupt an ecosystem in a different way.

It is time to correct this deficit in the EPA by bringing to the forefront policy mechanisms to protect essential ecological functioning in agriculture. Our society depends on this occurring, and we will not see a greener future without it. The EPA's Environmental Monitoring and Assessment Program has done a much better job of this on U.S. waterways than in agriculture.[19] Currently, the ecological impacts of pesticides are not realistically scaled against such other anthropological impacts as human sprawl, loss of wildlife corridors, industrialization, road construction, air pollution, water pollution, water channelization, and global warming.

Certainly the management and maintenance of open spaces are essential for the earth's ecological functioning and the future of humankind. This is especially true near water, as on the land along the western shore of Lake Michigan where tart cherries are produced. If current EPA policy is allowed to continue, formerly viable, ecologically invaluable agriculture such as the tart cherry industry in the Upper Midwest will quickly be swallowed by sprawl.

Notes

1. U.S. Environmental Protection Agency, "Federal Insecticide, Fungicide, and Rodenticide Act (FIFRA) Enforcement," http://www.epa.gov/oecaerth/civil/fifra/index.html.

2. M. T. Lambur, M. E. Whalon, and F. A. Fear, "Diffusion Theory and Integrated Pest Management: Illustrations from the Michigan Fruit IPM Program," *Bulletin of the ESA* 31, no. 3 (1985): 40–45.

3. U.S. Food and Drug Administration, "Federal Food, Drug and Cosmetic Act," http://www.fda.gov/RegulatoryInformation/Legislation/FederalFoodDrugand CosmeticActFDCAct/default.htm.

4. U.S. Environmental Protection Agency, "Federal Insecticide, Fungicide, and Rodenticide Act, Amended 2008," http://agriculture.senate.gov/Legislation/Compilations/Fifra/FIFRA.pdf; U.S. Food and Drug Administration, "Federal Food, Drug and Cosmetic Act, Significant Amendments," http://www.fda.gov/RegulatoryInformation/Legislation/FederalFoodDrugandCosmeticActFDCAct/SignificantAmenSignificantAmendm/default.htm.

5. E. C. Brown et al., *The Environmental Law Reporter Pesticide Regulation Deskbook* (Washington, DC: Environmental Law Institute, 2000)

6. U.S. Environmental Protection Agency, "Food Quality Protection Act (FQPA)," http://www.epa.gov/agriculture/lqpa.html.

7. Food and Agriculture Organization/World Health Organization, "Codex Alimentarius: Pesticide Residues in Food," http://www.codexalimentarius.net/mrls/pestdes/jsp/pest_q-e.jsp.

8. M. E. Whalon, D. Epstein, D. Alston, et al., "Reduced Risk Pest Management Systems for U.S. Tart Cherry Production—Risk Avoidance and Mitigation Project (RAMP) I" (6th International IPM Symposium, Portland, Oregon, 2009).

9. U.S. Department of Agriculture, National Agricultural Statistics Service, "Cherry Production," http://usda.mannlib.cornell.edu/usda/nass/CherProd//2000s/2009/ CherProd-06-18-2009.pdf.

10. "Michigan Fruit Management Guide 2008," *Michigan State University Extension Bulletin* (2008): E-154; M. E. Whalon, D. Epstein, L. Gut, et al., "Functional Ecology: A Catalyst for Change in Tree Fruit IPM," *IPM Report* 12, no. 1 (2006).

11. Michigan State University/Michigan Department of Agriculture, "FQPA-Targeted Pesticide Residue Study," 1999, http://www.ipm.msu.edu/pdf/FQPA TargetedResidueReport.pdf.

12. Whalon, Epstein, Alston, et al., "Reduced Risk Pest Management Systems."

13. M. E. Whalon and J. Wise, "Biorational Integration, Resistance Management, and Ecological Assessment in Tree Fruit Orchards" (6th International IPM Symposium, Portland, Oregon, 2009).

14. Federal Insecticide, Fungicide, and Rodenticide Act 346a(b)(2)(B)(iii), http://agriculture.senate.gov/Legislation/Compilations/Fifra/FIFRA.pdf.

15. Docket ID: EPA-HQ-OPP-2005-0061-0071.1, Comment Attachment Submitted by Cherry Marketing Institute to Azinphosmethyl Ecological Assessment, Grower Impact Assessments; Notice of Availability, February 2006, http://www.regulations.gov/search/Regs/home.html#documentDetail?R=09000064801270d9.

16. John Wargo, *Pesticides and Precaution?* (Washington, DC: American Enterprise Institute, 2009).

17. Committee on Pesticides in the Diets of Infants and Children, Board on Agriculture and Board on Environmental Studies and Toxicology, *Pesticides in the Diets of Infants and Children* (Washington, DC: National Academy Press, 1993).

18. M. E. Whalon and B. A. Croft, "Immigration and Colonization of Portable Apple Trees by Arthropod Pests and Their Natural Enemies," *Crop Protection* 5 (1986): 376–84.

19. U.S. Environmental Protection Agency, "Environmental Monitoring and Assessment Program," http://www.epa.gov/emap/.

5

Unintended Consequences: Dangerous Misconceptions about Public Health Insecticides, the Environment, and Human Health

Richard Tren

Though many Americans may face a restless night's sleep worrying about paying the mortgage or meeting work deadlines, hardly any will lie awake worrying that they may face severe illness and possible death if they happen to be bitten by a mosquito. Mosquitoes may be abundant and annoying in the United States, but they no longer transmit malaria. The fact that this disease no longer threatens Americans is thanks in large part to the judicious use of public health insecticides several decades ago. Many millions of Africans and poor people living in Latin America and Southeast Asia unfortunately do face the threat of debilitating insect-borne diseases such as malaria. Malaria snatches young children from their mother's arms, kills pregnant women, and keeps people out of productive work. Every year, malaria kills close to a million people, mostly African children, and estimates suggest that it robs some African countries of as much as 1.3 percent growth in GDP annually.[1] Yet malaria and many other insect-borne diseases, such as yellow fever and dengue, are preventable. Unfortunately, the tools to prevent these diseases, which rely mostly on insecticides, have been subject to orchestrated and well-funded campaigns to limit their use. This means not only that people in poor countries presently lack sufficient protection from disease-carrying insects but also that research into new, much-needed chemicals for future use has been discouraged.

A popular image of insecticide use is of an aerial sprayer, dusting crops with a fine white powder. Most people perceive these chemicals to be harmful, threatening their health and welfare, even where there is no evidence of actual harm. Unfortunately, very few realize that insecticides play a crucial role in public health, protecting people from deadly insects without causing harm to human health. Most insect-borne diseases, such as malaria, are complex and difficult to control. These diseases involve pathogens such as parasites or viruses, insects such as mosquitoes or sand flies, and human populations. The strategies to control these types of diseases vary from place to place and depend on climate, geography, disease-spreading vector (insect), and human behavior. One common element to almost all successful vector-borne disease programs over the past one hundred years or so has been the use of effective insecticides.

Yet despite the lifesaving role that these chemicals play, there is remarkably little investment, either public or private, in finding new and effective insecticides. The spread of insecticide resistance has reduced the utility of some insecticides, which exposes populations to increased risk of disease. Unlike vaccines and medicines, which are also essential in controlling disease, public health insecticides do not benefit from legisla-tion or public policies that would stimulate innovation and research. The public, particularly in Western countries, often have a knee-jerk aversion to insecticides and have little appreciation of the role that these agents play in saving lives.

Over the past thirty years, government regulations have made develop-ing and using man-made chemicals much more expensive and difficult. It is important to assess the actual and potential hazards of various chemicals and to balance their utility against potential harms. Regulations may have been created to protect the environment and human health. However, some regulations do not address scientific and health risks, but have been put in place for ideological reasons in response to advocacy campaigns. This has led to reduced investment, fewer chemicals to control deadly insects, and the curtailing of the use of insecticides known to be effective in disease-control programs. The most striking target has been DDT (dichlorodiphenyl-trichloroethane), an insecticide that has become the totemic villain of the environmental movement, yet has probably saved more lives from malaria and other diseases than any other chemical. Understanding the mistakes made during the banning of DDT is essential if we are to improve insecticide policies and bring new, safe, and effective insecticides to market.

According to a well-known idiom, prevention is better than cure. This is also true for insect-borne diseases. The only proven and consistent method of insect-borne disease prevention (where vaccines do not exist and where drug prophylaxis is undesirable or too expensive) is vector control—suppressing contact between disease-spreading vectors (mosquitoes, flies, lice, and other insects) and humans in order to interrupt disease transmission.

Combined, the insect-borne diseases malaria, dengue, leishmaniasis, filariasis, and yellow fever infect an estimated four hundred million people or more every year.[2] Yellow fever is the only major insect-borne disease for which an effective vaccine is currently in use. But even when a vaccine is available and effective, insufficient vaccination rates can lead to disease outbreaks that require vector control for containment. The 2008 outbreak of yellow fever in Brazil is evidence of the importance of sustaining comprehensive disease-control programs that include robust vector control.[3]

Insecticides remain the most important element in vector control for malaria and other important insect-borne diseases. Indoor residual spraying (IRS) (the process of applying small amounts of insecticide to the inside walls of houses) and insecticide-treated bed nets, including long-lasting insecticidal nets, are proven vector control interventions that rely heavily on safe, effective, and long lasting insecticides.

Only twelve insecticides, from four different chemical classes (organochlorines, organophosphates, pyrethroids, and carbamates), are currently recommended by the World Health Organization for IRS.[4] The oldest classes of these insecticides are the organochlorines, of which DDT is the only approved insecticide, and organophosphates, which are derived from phosphoric acid and have been used since the 1940s. The more modern pyrethroids are synthetic versions of the naturally occurring pyrethrum insecticide, which is derived from the chrysanthemum flower. Six pyrethroid insecticides are authorized for use in vector control. Two carbamates, a more modern class of insecticide, are recommended for use in IRS.

Because all classes of public health insecticides, with the exception of organochlorines, are still used in the agricultural sector, vector species (such as mosquitoes, flies, lice, and other insects) experience prolonged exposure to the chemicals. The widespread use of insecticides for agricultural and public health purposes increases the probability that resistance will develop. When vectors breed in proximity to agricultural crops, they are exposed to the same or similar insecticidal compounds, and thus resistant genes may be driven through insect populations.[5] Many vector species of public health importance have developed resistance to one or more insecticides.[6]

Insecticide resistance poses a major threat to vector control. Mosquitoes' prolonged exposure to an insecticide over several generations increases their ability to survive after coming into contact with that insecticide. Mosquitoes can produce many generations per year, allowing resistance to develop quickly. In some cases, insecticide resistance has been documented within just a few years of the insecticide being introduced. Within the four chemical classes, the mode of action, or the way in which the chemical functions to either kill or repel the insect, will be broadly similar. This means that if a resistant gene emerges to a pyrethroid product, for instance, and is driven through a population, there will likely be resistance to all pyrethroids.

In light of recent calls to massively scale up the distribution of insecticide-treated bed nets and long-lasting insecticidal nets, pyrethroid resistance is of particular concern. Increased resistance would inhibit the effectiveness of this intervention by allowing mosquitoes to enter and/or bite through the nets. There is growing concern that extensive use of insecticide-treated bed nets and long-lasting insecticidal nets could contribute to the spread of insecticide resistance.[7]

For these reasons, the development of new chemical classes with different modes of action is important for sustained disease control. Yet according to the Insecticide Resistance Action Committee, "The most recent 'new' compound made available for vector use is etofenprox (a pyrethroid) which was commercialized in 1986, and even this did not possess a distinct mode of action." Furthermore, the public health and agricultural sectors require insecticides with substantially different properties and modes of chemical action.[8] Agricultural insecticides are designed to be short acting and have a narrow activity spectrum, whereas public health insecticides need long-lasting residual action and a broader spectrum of chemical activity. Agricultural insecticides will tend to act on the insect's stomach after it has ingested a crop, while public health insecticides will act as a contact poison after the insect has landed on a wall or other material.

DDT—Setting the Stage for the Anti-Insecticides Movement

DDT is different from other insecticides in key ways. It was not developed for public health, but was discovered in the search for a chemical to control clothes moths. Its first use in public health was during World War II when it was used to control human lice that spread typhus. Lice-spread typhus had plagued armies and civilians for centuries, thriving in the unsanitary and often crowded conditions of war. During World War II, typhus claimed many thousands of lives, including diarist Anne Frank after she was imprisoned in Bergen-Belsen. Yet with DDT the disease-spreading pests finally met their match. DDT powder was doused on civilians and soldiers alike and dusted in clothes and bed linen. A typhus epidemic following the Allied liberation of Naples was controlled within just a few short weeks after U.S. troops doused more than 1.3 million people with DDT. DDT demonstrated its value against not only lice but also malaria-spreading mosquitoes, and, as a result, the Allies sprayed DDT inside houses and barracks in the Pacific Theater to contain malaria epidemics.

DDT was the first long-lasting insecticide to be used in public health. Previously, chemicals such as natural pyrethrum remained effective for around two weeks, whereas DDT, when sprayed on walls, would last for up to a year. The low cost of DDT and its long-lasting effect meant that malaria-control programs could be greatly expanded, providing protection to many millions of people. Since its introduction to disease control, DDT has been hailed by almost all public health scientists as a remarkable chemical and the most successful public health insecticide in history.

Even after decades of public health use, DDT is still one of the best chemicals for preventing malaria transmission inside houses. Although resistance to DDT's toxic action (that is, the killing action when mosquitoes rest on a DDT-sprayed surface) has been noted, this resistance developed mostly as a result of DDT use in agriculture, not in public health. Even where DDT resistance exists, the chemical still has a very valuable public health role because the primary and most important way in which DDT acts is as a spatial repellent, keeping mosquitoes out of homes and away from people. In the same way that a mesh window screen stops mosquitoes from entering houses, so DDT acts as a chemical screen. This repellency prevents the selection of resistant genes in mosquitoes when used for malaria control.[9] In fact, DDT is the only chemical recommended for malaria control that stops mosquitoes from entering houses and thus transmitting disease.[10] This repellency was observed by early users of DDT, and it has been repeatedly documented in the scientific literature for several decades.[11]

DDT's remarkable success in saving lives was not welcomed by all. Growing concern in the 1960s about increasing human populations and the impact that increase might have on natural resource availability and the environment caused some prominent activists and writers, such as Paul Ehrlich, to rail against DDT. Ehrlich campaigned against the "export of death control" so that poor countries could stop unnecessary deaths from preventable diseases.[12] This remarkably callous attitude to human suffering was apparently well accepted. Concerns about DDT's impact on the environment, and particularly on birds, led to the greatest opposition to its use and resulted in its eventual banning. DDT's widespread use in agriculture meant that it was sprayed aerially in large quantities, and DDT residues were found in fields, wetlands, rivers, and streams and accumulated in the fatty tissues of animals. Concerns about the effects DDT would have on animals led one writer, Rachel Carson, to predict a world without birds and their songs, resulting in a silent spring, which was the emotive title of her best-selling book. Carson also claimed that DDT would lead to various human health problems, including cancers. However, these fears, and Carson's claims about DDT's harm to bird populations and human health, were simply wrong.

Dangerous Misperceptions—DDT and Wildlife

There are many popular misconceptions about the alleged harmfulness of DDT. It is generally perceived that widespread use of DDT led to the demise of the bald eagle in the United States and that the subsequent banning of DDT resulted in the eagles' recovery. At high doses, DDT can cause eggshell thin-ning, and crushed bird eggs would kill chicks and harm bird populations. Yet a closer look at the history of the bald eagle provides a different conclusion.

For centuries, hunting of bald eagles was widespread. Eagles were shot for sport, meat, and feathers. They were also poisoned by farmers because they threatened livestock. Changes in land use also contributed to the decline in bald eagle populations. In fact, bald eagles were threat-ened and driven almost to extinction long before DDT was ever used in the United States.

The Eagle Protection Act was passed in 1940 in an attempt to protect the bald eagle, but the act was poorly enforced due to a lack of funding. There was also no funding available to reintroduce bald eagles to areas where they had been previously eliminated. To add to this, the juvenile bald eagle is indistinguishable from the golden eagle. The Eagle Protection Act did not protect golden eagles, and, being indistinguishable, juvenile bald eagles were shot in spite of the act's existence. After 1940, selective shoot-ing of juvenile bald eagles caused a relative decline in juvenile compared to adult bald eagles.

In 1962, the Eagle Protection Act was amended to include golden eagles. The amendment not only protected golden eagles but also pre-vented the shooting of juvenile bald eagles, and the act was strictly enforced. Improved survival of juveniles led to increasing numbers of both juvenile and breeding pairs of bald eagles. The Endangered Species Act of 1973 provided additional funding, permitting the creation of programs to reintroduce fledgling eaglets to previous nesting areas. This act, along with enforcement of the amended Eagle Protection Act, allowed nesting pairs of bald eagles to recover even more quickly than in the 1960s. The U.S. Fish and Wildlife Service recorded 417 pairs of bald eagles in 1963 and 791 in 1974. This doubling of nesting pairs of eagles occurred even as environmentalists were claiming bald eagle populations were in steep decline due to DDT contamination. Nesting pairs of bald eagles in the United States had increased greatly even before the DDT ban came into effect in January 1973.

DDT was accused of harming not only eagles but peregrine falcons as well. Yet, historically, man has been a far more serious danger to raptors than has DDT. Eagles, falcons, and other raptors have not always been romanticized as they are in today's culture. People's perception of raptors has changed dramatically over the decades. As in the case of eagles, falcons were once routinely hunted or taken by falconers. An example of how perceptions have changed can be found in the 1935 edition of *Hornaday's American Natural History*. Because falcons fed on songbirds, people who valued songbirds were encouraged to kill falcons. Hornaday reported that nine of twenty falcons examined had fed on songbirds—birds that he was fond of. He described his solution to the falcon problem in graphic detail: "It can best be studied with a rope, a basket, and a chokebore shot-gun loaded with No. 6 shot. First shoot both male and female birds, then collect the nest, and the eggs or young, whichever may be present."[13]

So although large quantities of DDT can certainly harm eggshells, a more balanced evaluation of wildlife history in the United States shows that direct action by man, such as hunting, poisoning, and changes in land use, are likely to have played a much more important role in the decline of certain species, such as the bald eagle and peregrine falcon. Furthermore, the subsequent rise in populations of these species may well have had less to do with the banning of DDT and more to do with specific legislation designed to protect the species, as well as actions to reintroduce breeding pairs.

The EPA Takes on DDT

With growing wealth and prosperity in the United States during the twentieth century, Americans were able to afford the luxury of showing concern for the natural environment. Awareness of and appreciation for nature increase with prosperity, and with DDT successfully, though incorrectly, characterized as leading to great environmental harm, pressure to ban the insecticide started to rise. In the late 1960s, several legal actions were launched against state governments to ban DDT, resulting from increased sales of the book *Silent Spring* and public support for environmental lobby groups and legal groups such as the Environmental Defense Fund. The most significant legal action was brought before the newly established Environmental Protection Agency in 1972.

The EPA's DDT hearings lasted around eight months, featured expert testimony from 125 witnesses both for and against DDT, and resulted in a transcript of more than nine thousand pages. The hearing examiner, Judge Edmund Sweeney, filed his opinion in April 1972, recommending that DDT not be banned:

> DDT is not a carcinogenic hazard to man. DDT is not a mutagenic or teratogenic hazard to man. The uses of DDT under the registration involved here do not have a deleterious effect on freshwater fish, estuarine organisms, wild birds or other wildlife. The adverse effect on beneficial animals from the use of DDT under the registrations involved here is not unreasonable on balance with its benefit. The use of DDT in the United States has declined rapidly since 1959. The Petitioners have met fully their burden of proof. There is a present need for the continued use of DDT for the essential uses defined in this case.[14]

Yet two months later, on June 2, 1972, the EPA's administrator, William D. Ruckelshaus, issued his opinion, ignoring the results of the hearing and canceling all uses of DDT for crop production and nonhealth purposes in the United States.[15] In his opinion he implied that DDT was toxic to humans. Although the EPA reserved the use of DDT for emergencies, particularly public health emergencies, this ban effectively ended the use of DDT in the United States and compromised its use around the world.[16]

Although scientists defended DDT, the industry response was not robust. As Robert Desowitz, a leading epidemiologist, explains:

> There were few defenders of DDT; the agricultural chemical industry actually welcomed the opportunity to abandon DDT. It was too cheap, and newer, much more expensive and profitable pesticides were ready for the farmer's market....Giving up DDT made the industry look self-righteous, that they were working for the best interest of humans and nature. There was no dissent when, in 1972, the newly created Environmental Protection Agency (EPA) banned the use of DDT.[17]

In an extraordinary move, the EPA recommended a replacement for DDT, methyl parathion, which was actually more toxic to humans than DDT.

There had been several deaths from accidental poisoning with methyl parathion, yet there had never been any recorded deaths or even human illness from environmental exposure to DDT (nor have there been since). The EPA was aware of both of these facts and had to allow a six-month waiting period before the order would come into effect so that the USDA and the EPA could train operators of spraying equipment and others on how to use this more dangerous insecticide.[18]

In 1975, the EPA submitted an assessment to the U.S. House of Representatives of the scientific and economic aspects of its decision to delist DDT for use in agriculture. In its assessment of poisonings associated with accidental exposures to parathion and methyl parathion, they found that

> parathion and methyl parathion are the pesticides most frequently cited in incidents involving accidental exposure to pesticides. Preliminary data from the EPA Pesticide Accident Surveillance System (PASS) shows that parathion is the third and methyl parathion is the fifth most frequently cited pesticide in 1973. Based on an analysis of PASS data, Osmun (1974) stated that for 1972 and 1973, parathion and/or methyl parathion were connected with 78% of the reported episodes relating to agricultural jobs, particularly those involving fields sprayed with pesticides for which safe reentry times for workers had been set.[19]

It is surely a measure of how successful environmental campaigners had been in vilifying DDT that the EPA would replace this relatively safe and benign chemical with one so toxic to humans.

The hastily reached politicized decision to ban DDT continued to haunt the public health community. Then, twenty-seven years after promoting methyl parathion as a substitute for DDT, the EPA finally came to terms with its risks. The agency accepted voluntary cancellation of many registered uses of methyl parathion in 1999 with an assessment that "methyl parathion is hazardous to workers—people who handle or apply the pesticide as part of their occupation, and people who work in fields to harvest treated crops. Protective clothing and equipment are not sufficient to reduce the risks to workers to acceptable levels."[20] History has proved that Judge Sweeney was correct—DDT is not a human carcinogen, and the primary replacement insecticide was truly more dangerous than DDT.

DDT and Human Health

Fears about DDT's impacts on human health have continued to mount, despite a lack of credible evidence. DDT has been accused of causing almost every imaginable human health problem. In May 2009, *Environmental Health Perspectives* published "The Pine River Statement: Human Health Consequences of DDT Use."[21] The statement, written by fifteen scientists from the United States and South Africa, summarizes information on the health risks of DDT use and makes recommendations for public health policy. Overall, the Pine River Statement presents no new or compelling evidence that DDT or its metabolite, dichlorodiphenyldichloroethylene (DDE), is a cause of impaired human health. The evidence presented is weak and sometimes contradictory, and it fails to meet the basic epidemiological criteria to prove a cause-and-effect relationship; frequently, the studies cited are scientifically unreplicated, present statistically insignificant and weak correlations, or fail the criterion of consistency across studies.

Most recently, a study published in the *British Journal of Urology International* claimed that DDT house spraying would increase the chances of a male being born with a urogenital birth defect (UGBD) by 33 percent.[22] This alarming statistic has been picked up by media around the world, particularly in South Africa, where the study was conducted and where DDT is still being used successfully to control malaria. Closer examination of the paper reveals problems with the interpretation and representation of cited literature, as well as several inconsistencies and shortcomings in design, data analyses, and interpretation.[23] The authors of the study claim that DDT is a cause of UGBDs, but in fact, as with the studies cited in the Pine River Statement, they fail to satisfy even the most basic epidemiological requirements to prove cause and effect. The study reports the percentage of UGBDs in boys born in villages where DDT is used in IRS as 11 percent (extremely high given a global average of around 2 percent). Yet the study also found that the percentage of UGBDs in boys born in villages where DDT was never used in IRS was 10.2 percent, very close to 11 percent. Although UGBDs are no doubt a serious problem, it is highly unlikely that DDT is the cause, and the study amounts to a distraction from finding the real cause of UGBDs. Equally worrying is that the wide promotion of the study's findings in the media in southern Africa has reportedly raised fears about DDT in malaria-control programs in rural areas. This has the potential to hamper malaria-control efforts and increase the risk of disease and possible death to vulnerable populations.

DDT Use Globally

During the time DDT was banned from use in agriculture, the EPA ruling and subsequent rulings from other regulators around the world permitted its use in public health programs. Yet the agricultural ban led to a rise in the price of DDT, making the task of obtaining sufficient quantities for malaria control increasingly difficult. In 1971, the Indonesian representative to the World Health Assembly remarked that the price of DDT had increased by around $50 a ton over two years (an increase of around 10 percent).[24] A 1972 WHO report on proposed program and budget estimates stated, "A member pointed out that DDT was still the insecticide used for eradication programs in most countries. However, certain countries had stopped manufacturing DDT and some Member States were experiencing difficulties in obtaining the required supplies."[25] Over the years that followed the ban, persistent campaigns against DDT continued, focusing on the elimination of not only DDT but also all public health insecticides.

These campaigns have seriously impacted the public health of the world's poor. Data from Latin America showed that as house-spraying rates declined, malaria cases rose.[26] However, the rising rates of malaria around the world, and the lack of proven alternatives to insecticides, did not stop the World Health Assembly from passing a resolution in 1997 calling on member states to reduce their reliance on insecticides for disease control.[27] During the discussion and debate of the resolution at the WHO executive board meeting in January 1997, the chairman of the session called on Consumers International, a group designated to represent the interests of Western consumers and known to be hostile about DDT, to make arguments in favor of the resolution and against the use of DDT in disease control. There is no record that WHO permitted testimony from scientists involved in insect-borne disease control, disease-control program managers, or citizens of the countries affected by insect-borne diseases.[28]

Pressure against the use of DDT continued until 2006, when Dr. Arata Kochi was appointed head of WHO's Global Malaria Program and announced that he was supporting the use of DDT.[29] Despite the fact that a new global partnership among WHO, UNICEF, the World Bank, and other leading donors, known as Roll Back Malaria (RBM), had been established in 1998 with the lofty goal of halving the burden of malaria by 2010, little progress had been made against the disease. With growing criticism of WHO and RBM from some scientists and advocacy groups and increasingly bad press for RBM, WHO director general Dr. J. W. Lee appointed Dr. Kochi to "clean house" and reform malaria control.[30] Dr. Kochi was an outsider to the malaria community and had not been associated with any previous policies to limit insecticide use. Although WHO had never officially argued against DDT, WHO leadership in Geneva had certainly not backed it, and until then almost all support for malaria control was restricted to the use of insecticide-treated bed nets, rather than indoor residue spraying. In September 2006, soon after his appointment, Dr. Kochi gave the following press statement:

> I asked my staff; I asked malaria experts around the world: "Are we using every possible weapon to fight this disease?" It became apparent that we were not. One powerful weapon against malaria was not being deployed. In a battle to save the lives of nearly one million children every year—most of them in Africa— the world was reluctant to spray the inside of houses and huts with insecticides; especially with a highly effective insecticide known as *dichlorodiphenyltricloroethane* or "DDT."[31]

Dr. Kochi promoted a more comprehensive approach to malaria control, which included IRS and DDT. Predictably, Dr. Kochi's statements on DDT drew howls of disapproval from many environmentalist groups, such as the Pesticide Action Network (PAN).[32]

Anti-Insecticides Movement

Although some countries have restarted IRS programs with funding from the U.S. government, no country has started using DDT that had not used it in the past. In fact, some countries that have wanted to start using DDT have been thwarted in their efforts. For example, as early as 2004, the Ugandan government had announced that, on the basis of Uganda's past success with DDT spraying and other African countries' current successes, it would begin an IRS program using DDT. Unfortunately, the announcement triggered an astonishing campaign to stop the use of DDT, led by some environmentalists and organic farmers. One such environmental activist and politician—Ken Lukyamuzi—told crowds that the government was spraying DDT in order to kill them and that DDT would cause liver cancer, blindness, brain damage, and kidney failure. He went on to incite people to violence, instructing them, "Get your saw, your machete, your axe! Greet the spraymen at your house."[33]

To make matters worse, the European Union warned the Ugandan government that any traces of DDT on any exported produce to Europe would lead to its rejection. This decision did not take into account sound science or evidence that DDT reduces malaria deaths (the leading cause of death among children in Uganda) and resulted in pitting the agricultural sector against the health sector. Regardless, the government started spraying with help from the United States Agency for International Development (USAID), and malaria cases began to fall, by 20 percent in one district and 40 percent in another. The government was then sued by a coalition of agricultural exporters. In an assessment by the Research Triangle Institute—the USAID contractor that undertook the spraying—traces of DDT were found on coffee. This likely would have been due to the storage of coffee inside sprayed houses, but not because DDT was misappropriated and sprayed on trees or fields. Fifty-five percent of samples had traces of DDT, at concentrations ranging between 0.011 and 0.26 mg/kg. Even at the highest recorded level, the amount of DDT that a European consumer would be exposed to if he or she drank two to three cups of coffee would be 12,000 times below the no-observable-effect level based on long-term dosing experiments on humans. Nonetheless, the IRS program was terminated, malaria returned, and lives were lost.

Many organizations peddle fears about man-made chemicals, seemingly oblivious to the fact that the risks of not using these chemicals are far greater than the risks of using them. This line of thinking goes back to the original decision by William Ruckelshaus in 1972 to ban DDT. In its own description of the agency and its history, the EPA itself admits it was an activist decision: "Though unpopular among certain segments of EPA's constituency, his [Ruckelshaus's] decision did serve to enhance the activist image he sought to create for the agency, and without prohibitive political cost."[34]

Are There Effective Alternatives to Insecticides?

This anti-chemical agenda has limited new investment in insecticides for public health. There exist generous state-funded programs to find new vaccines and medicines for malaria and other tropical diseases, but almost no funding for public health insecticides, which are as important, if not more so. Aside from a laudable $50 million grant from the Bill and Melinda Gates Foundation to the Innovative Vector Control Consortium, no new investment of any significance has been made in the search for public health insecticides.

Organizations such as PAN advocate for malaria prevention methods such as improved sanitation and water drainage as alternatives to chemical spraying and to the use of DDT in particular.[35] PAN cites case studies in Mexico and Kenya as possible safe and effective solutions to malaria.[36] Mexico used "pharmacosuppression" to control malaria.[37] In 2005, Mexico had reported only 2,967 cases of malaria, yet the country dispensed more than eight million tablets of chloroquine and/or amodiaquine.[38] With just 2,967 cases, the statistics reveal that a large number of people in Mexico were given malaria treatment who had almost no chance of contracting the disease. Antiparasitic agents are toxic and biologically active in divers ways, and in contrast to public health insecticides, they are ingested. Humans have been known to die of malaria treatment tablets, although such occurrences are rare. There have been no documented human deaths or illnesses from environmental exposures to DDT.

The project cited by PAN in Kenya proposed using improved water management, biological control, insecticide-treated bed nets, and livestock as bait to control malaria. The case study stated, "The cattle would divert the blood-seeking mosquitoes away from humans."[39] The desire of PAN and other environmentalist groups to replace pesticide use with "ecologically sound and socially just alternatives" may resonate well with some who are anxious about the use of man-made chemicals.[40] However, such approaches usually focus on the potential risk posed by man-made chemicals and ignore the very real and deadly risks posed by disease-spreading insects.

Calls for what their proponents refer to as "ecologically sound" methods of malaria control are not new. A 1979 report by the WHO Expert Committee on Malaria discusses progress in developing biological controls such as larvivorous fish, microbial agents, genetic control, and environmental management. Despite the somewhat optimistic assessment of these alternative methods, however, these technologies remain unproven and are very limited in their usefulness for malaria control, which still relies on man-made chemicals for vector control.

Conclusion

Whether intended or unintended, campaigns against man-made chemicals have successfully shut down IRS programs, limited new investment in alternative chemicals, and cost human lives. The EPA's decision in 1972 to ban DDT was based not on science or risk assessment but on politics. As the EPA itself acknowledges, the banning of DDT was an activist decision.

As a result of this anti-insecticides activism, public health professionals have fewer available tools to fight insect-borne diseases, which in many countries are of growing importance. The current push is for malaria eradication. However, this can never happen without effective tools and investment, which requires a shift in the thinking and recognition that just like medicines and vaccines, insecticides save lives. Political champions, smart legislation to reward private investment, and public investment similar to that for vaccines are sorely needed.

Notes

1. John Luke Gallup and Jeffrey D. Sachs, "The Economic Burden of Malaria," *American Journal of Tropical Medicine and Hygiene* 64 (2001): 85–96.

2. Ibid.; World Health Organization, "Dengue and Dengue Hemorrhagic Fever," http://www.who.int/mediacentre/factsheets/fs117/en/; World Health Organization, "Yellow Fever," http://www.who.int/mediacentre/factsheets/fs100/en/; World Health Organization, "Leishmaniasis Burden of Disease," http://www.who.int/leishmaniasis/burden/en/; World Health Organization, "Lymphatic Filariasis," http://www.who.int/mediacentre/factsheets/fs102/en/.

3. World Health Organization, "Global Alert and Response: Yellow Fever in Brazil," http://www.who.int/csr/don/2008_02_07/en/index.html.

4. World Health Organization, "WHO recommended insecticides for indoor residual spraying against malaria vectors," http://www.who.int/whopes/Insecticides_ IRS_Malaria_09.pdf   (accessed September 22, 2010).

5. Insecticide Resistance Action Committee, "Why Effective Insecticide Resistance Management Is Important," http://www.irac-online.org/documents/importance_of_irm.pdf; World Health Organization, "Seventeenth Report of the WHO Expert Committee on Malaria," *Technical Report Series* 640 (1979): 49.

6. Insecticide Resistance Action Committee, "Why Effective Insecticide Resistance Management Is Important."

7. R. John, T. Ephraim, and A. Andrew, "Reduced Susceptibility to Pyrethroid Insecticide Treated Nets by the Malaria Vector *Anopheles gambiae s.l.* in Western Uganda," *Malaria Journal* 7, no. 92 (2008), http://www.malariajournal.com/content/7/1/92.

8. Insecticide Resistance Action Committee, "Prevention and Management of Insecticide Resistance in Vectors and Pests of Public Health Importance," http://www.irac-online.org/documents/vectormanual.pdf.

9. J. Grieco et al., "A New Classification System for the Actions of IRS Chemicals Traditionally Used for Malaria Control," *PLoS ONE* 2 , no. 8 (2007), http://www.plosone.org/article/info:doi%2F10.1371%2Fjournal.pone.0000716.

10. Ibid.

11. Donald Roberts and Richard Tren, *The Excellent Powder: DDT's Political and Scientific History* (Indianapolis: Dog Ear Publishing, 2010), 41–100.

12. Paul Ehrlich, *The Population Bomb* (Cutchogue, NY: Buccaneer Books, 1971), 15.

13. William Hornaday, *Hornaday's American Natural History*, 16th ed. (New York: Charles Scribner's Sons, 1935), 228.

14. E. Sweeney, "EPA Hearing Examiner's Recommendations and Findings concerning DDT Hearings," *Federal Register* (40 CFR 164.32), April 25, 1972.

15. U.S. Environmental Protection Agency, Environmental Appeals Board, *In the Matter of Stevens Industries, Inc., et al. before the Administrator, U.S. Environmental Protection Agency; Opinion by William D. Ruckelshaus*, Consolidated DDT Hearings, I.F. & R. Docket Nos. 63, et al. (June 2, 1972).

16. Other governments, especially European ones, had already banned the use of DDT.

17. Robert Desowitz, *Federal Bodysnatchers and the New Guinea Virus*, 1st ed. (New York: W. W. Norton, 2002), 64.

18. U.S. Environmental Protection Agency, *In the Matter of Stevens Industries*.

19. U.S. Environmental Protection Agency, *DDT: A Review of Scientific and Economic Aspects of the Decision to Ban Its Use as a Pesticide*, prepared for Committee on Appropriations, U.S. House of Representatives, Washington, DC, July 1975.

20. U.S. Environmental Protection Agency, "Methyl Parathion Risk Management Decision" http://www.epa.gov/pesticides/factsheets/chemicals/mpfactsheet.htm.

21. B. Eskenazi et al., "The Pine River Statement: Human Health Consequences of DDT Use," *Environmental Health Perspectives* 117, no. 9 (2009): 1359–67, http://www.ehponline.org/members/2009/11748/11748.pdf.

22. R. Bornman et al., "DDT and Urogenital Malformations in Newborn Boys in a Malarial Area," *BJU International* (2009), http://www.ncbi.nlm.nih.gov/pubmed/19849691.

23. For specific examples, see Africa Fighting Malaria's response to the paper, http://www.fightingmalaria.org/pdfs/responsebornmanetal.pdf.

24. World Health Organization, 24th World Health Assembly, Part 2, Official WHO Records, 1971, no. 194, p. 366, Pan American Health Organization Library, Washington, DC.

25. World Health Organization, Executive Board, 49th Session, Part 2, Official WHO Records, 1972, no. 198, Report on the Proposed Programme and Budget Estimates for 1973—chapter 2, p. 23, Pan American Health Organization Library, Washington, DC.

26. D. Roberts et al., "DDT, Global Strategies, and a Malaria Control Crisis in South America," *Emerging Infectious Diseases* 3, no. 3 (1997): 295-302.

27. World Health Organization, "The International Programme on Chemical Safety: World Health Assembly Resolution 50.13," http://www.who.int/ipcs/publications/wha/whares_53_13/en/index.html.

28. World Health Organization, Executive Board Ninety-ninth Session: Provisional Summary Record of the Sixteenth Meeting, 1997, pp. 14–17, Pan American Health Organization Library, Washington, DC.

29. World Health Organization, "WHO Gives Indoor Use of DDT a Clean Bill of Health for Controlling Malaria," http://www.who.int/mediacentre/news/releases/2006/pr50/en/index.html.

30. A. Attaran, "Malaria: Where Did It All Go Wrong?" *Nature*, August 19, 2004, 932-33; G. Yamey, "Roll Back Malaria: A Failing Public Health Program," *British Medical Journal* 328 (2004): 1086–87.

31. World Health Organization, press statement by Dr. Arata Kochi, director of the World Health Organization's Malaria Department, September 15, 2006, National Press Club, Washington, DC, http://malaria.who.int/docs/KochiIRS Speech15Sep06.pdf.

32. Pesticide Action Network UK, "What's Behind the 'DDT Comeback'"? http://www.pan-uk.org/Info/DDT/comeback.html.

33. K. Lewis, "DDT Stalemate Stymies Malaria Control Initiative," *Canadian Medical Association Journal* 179, no. 10 (2008), http://www.cmaj.ca/cgi/content/full/179/10/999.

34. U.S. Environmental Protection Agency, "Pesticides and Public Health," http://www.epa.gov/history/publications/formative6.htm.

35. Pesticide Action Network North America, "Safe and Effective Solutions," http://www.panna.org/ddt/solutions.

36. Ibid.

37. International Development Research Centre, "Case Study: Mexico (Malaria)," http://www.idrc.ca/en/ev-29136-201-1-DO_TOPIC.html.

38. Pan American Health Organization, "Status of Malaria in the Americas, 1994–2007: A Series of Data Tables" (table 7: Antimalarial Drugs Used in 21 Countries in 2006; table 8: Antimalarial Treatment Completed in 2007), http://www.paho.org/English/AD/DPC/CD/mal-americas-2007.pdf.

39. International Development Research Centre, "Case Study: Kenya," http://www.idrc.ca/en/ev-29117-201-1-DO_TOPIC.html.

40. Pesticide Action Network North America, "About PAN North America," http://www.panna.org/about.

PART III

Precautionary Politics

6

Precaution, Custom, and the World Trade Organization

Claude Barfield

The goal of this chapter is to place the "precautionary principle" in the broader context of public international law and in the more specific context of evolving World Trade Organization (WTO) dispute settlement jurisprudence. The first section deals with the lack of defining principles underpinning the precautionary principle; the second discusses the recent history of customary international law (CIL); the third describes and analyzes decisions by WTO dispute panels relating to precaution and international law; and the fourth section describes the sweeping new European Union (EU) chemical regulations and the potential for international legal conflict over these new regulatory mandates. With its economic muscle and central role in international legal and regulatory bodies, the EU—now composed of twenty-seven separate nations, largely middle- and upper-income economies—is enjoying increasing success in pressing its own singular interpretation of the precautionary principle as the future global norm. The ensuing tale combines muddled definitions of the concept of the precautionary principle with a highly questionable process of international decision marking, resulting in a hopeless dilemma for WTO dispute settlement panels. In the future, however, it is quite possible that these WTO panels may be tempted to step into the breach and render judgments at this intersection of trade and the environment, despite the lack of a coherent rationale or clear body of precedent.

Precaution

At the most basic level, there is no agreed-upon definition of the precautionary principle, even among its most ardent proponents. It comes in many diverse iterations; one scholar has counted some nineteen different versions. An example of a so-called strong form definition is embodied in the Wingspread Statement of 1998: "When an activity raises threats of harm to human health or the environment, precautionary measures should be taken even if some cause and effect relationships are not fully established scientifically."[1] Similarly, the UN Biosafety Protocol justifies strong action merely from the "potential adverse effects" of diminishing biological diversity.[2] A third oft-cited and more qualified definition is found in Principle 15 of the 1992 Rio Declaration on Environment and Development: "In order to protect the environment, the *precautionary approach* shall be widely applied by States according to their capabilities. Where there are threats of serious and irreversible damage, lack of full scientific certainty shall not be used as a reason for postponing cost-effective measures to prevent environmental degradation."[3] This formulation bows in the direction of common sense by introducing "cost effectiveness" into the precautionary equation and by injecting a higher trigger of "serious and irreversible damage" to the environment.

As scholars Robert W. Hahn and Cass R. Sunstein have argued, however, even adopting the simplest interpretation, "better safe than sorry," leads inexorably to complex, unsolvable dilemmas. They query: "How safe is safe enough?" And they go on to point out: "For those who favor taking regulatory precautions, the conceptual difficulty is even worse. Risks, sometimes unforeseen, can arise from action as well as from inaction....And reducing risks in one policy domain (say, the environment) could increase risks in another (say, defense)—especially when resources are scarce." And finally they note: "A key problem with strong versions of the precautionary principle is that they are logically inconsistent. They would frequently eliminate *all* policies from consideration—including the status quo—because all policies impose risks of one kind or another."[4]

The lack of any clear agreement on definition has been central to the argument of the United States in WTO cases that "precaution" is not a rule of international law. As reported by a WTO panel: "According to the United States, the 'precautionary principle' cannot be considered a general principle or norm of international law because it does not have a single, agreed formulation. The United States notes in this regard that, on the contrary, the concept of precaution has many permutations across a number of different factors. Thus, the United States considers precaution to be an 'approach,' rather than a 'principle' of international law."[5]

Customary International Law

Despite the lack of definitional clarity, the EU argues that the precautionary principle has attained the status of customary international law and is therefore binding on all nations (*erga omnes*, in one of the Latin phrases so beloved of international legal scholars).[6] Just what is customary international law, and what is the validity of the EU's position?

There is a raging debate among legal scholars—and governments—as to just what constitutes the "law of custom" in the contemporary setting. Customary international law evolved during the eighteenth century and was generally considered to consist of general practices of nation states, or "what is habitually done by states out of a sense of legal obligation."[7] "Custom," as the noun implies, originally developed over a long period of time and pertained to such matters as rules of the sea, contraband, and piracy. Equally important, it was based on actual state practices and actions.

Thus matters stood for several centuries, but over the past few decades, a "new" international customary law has been espoused by some legal scholars, activists, and a few governments—notably the EU. Much of the purported new customary law has evolved from the soft law and hortatory declarations from UN bodies that, particularly from the 1980s, pronounced on such issues as the environment, human rights, women's rights, animal rights, racial discrimination, and so on—and on. Although court opinions may ultimately become the final arbiters on specific claims regarding "customary law," the construction of the case for such an evolution is based on sources far and wide—and suspect. Jeremy Rabkin, a critic of the contemporary evolution of customary international law, has described the evolution of this process:

> [Customary law] is not the product of court rulings, but of international conferences. Abstract pronouncements are enough. At that, they need not be authoritative pronouncements of supreme government authorities. Words spoken by diplomats at conference are given much weight, and then the reconfiguring of those words by commentators is supposed to give more weight, and the repetition of the words by yet other commentators is thought to lend still more weight to contentions about the law. Soon, there is a towering edifice of words, which is then treated as a secure marker of "customary international law."[8]

Scholars critical of the new theories regarding customary international law and domestic law point to the sharp difference between the process by which treaties are proposed, negotiated, and ratified by democratic states and the process defended by proponents of the new customary law. They point to intractable questions of legitimacy and democratic control. In an oft-cited article from the late 1990s, Curtis Bradley and Jack Goldsmith write:

> [The] modern position that CIL is federal common law is in tension with basic notions of American representative democracy. When a federal court applies CIL as federal common law, it is not applying law generated by the U.S. lawmaking processes. Rather, it is applying law derived from the views and practices of the international community. The foreign governments and other non-U.S. participants in this process "are neither representative of the American political community nor responsive to it." Indeed, under modern conceptions of CIL, CIL rules may be created and bind the United States without any express support for the rules from the U.S. political branches.[9]

They contrast this process with the traditional treaty-making process:

> Under U.S. practice, a treaty is a written document, negotiated and ratified by the President with the consent of the Senate,

and it is expressly made federal law by Article VI (of the constitution)....CIL is often unwritten and its contours are uncertain....Although these features reveal that CIL is much less grounded in American lawmaking processes than treaties, proponents of the modern position contend that all of CIL, unlike treaties, is "self-executing" federal law. This anomaly becomes even more troubling when one considers the changed nature of CIL....U.S. courts rely on multilateral treaties as a source of CIL, even in situations in which the United States has not ratified the treaty or has declared the relevant provisions of the treaty non-self-executing. In accordance with the modern position, these courts apply the norms derived from the treaties as self-executing federal common law. In other words, even when the political branches of the U.S. government have expressly declined to make the terms of a treaty part of U.S. law, the modern position permits, indeed requires, that courts do exactly that.[10]

These "anomalies" provoked Philip B. Trimble, a noted international legal theorist, to conclude: "The story of customary international law...does not fit the American political tradition....It is one thing to delegate authority to Congress and the President, checked and balanced by each other, and elected by different groups within the political constituency. But if customary international law can be made by practice wholly outside the United States, it has no basis in popular sovereignty at all."[11]

The World Trade Organization, the Precautionary Principle, and Customary International Law

The combination of the precautionary principle and customary international law has been tested and evaluated in several high-profile disputes since the creation of the WTO in 1995. The discussion and analysis herein will be confined to issues surrounding the famous EC–Hormones dispute that has pitted the EU against the United States and certain other WTO members. The analysis will also be confined to the substantive issues raised by the Sanitary and Phytosanitary Agreement (SPS) and Article XX(b) of the

General Agreement on Tariffs and Trade (GATT). (Article XX[b] sets forth exceptions to the general obligations under GATT for the protection of health and life.[12]) Succinctly, the EU invoked the SPS agreement, Article XX, and, ultimately, the precautionary principle and customary international law in defense of a ban on hormone-treated beef.

The SPS agreement will not be the main focus. It will be sufficient to give a brief account of its mandates, derived from the rules themselves and subsequent WTO cases. The SPS expressly recognizes the right of WTO members to take measures to protect human, animal, or plant life; but it also provides certain obligations, among which are: (1) measures may be imposed only to the extent necessary; (2) measures cannot be disguised barriers to trade; (3) measures cannot arbitrarily discriminate against WTO members; and (4) measures must constitute the least trade-restrictive means to achieve the protection. In addition, SPS measures must be based on international standards or guidelines, where such exist.[13]

Similarly, Article XX(b) allows WTO members to apply measures that would normally be contrary to the GATT so long as they do not arbitrarily discriminate against particular WTO members; they are not disguised protection; and they are necessary to protect human, animal, or plant life or health.

In both the beef hormones case and several subsequent challenges to the EU's ban on biotech products, WTO panels and the Appellate Body took up and attempted to answer a number of complex questions as to whether the EU had fulfilled the requirements noted above in the SPS agreement and Article XX(b). But of interest here, however, is the fact that the EU also based its decisions and defense of those decisions on the proposition that the precautionary principle has reached the status of customary international law and thus is binding on all nations.

In a 2000 "Communication from the Commission on the Precautionary Principle," the Commission of the European Communities (EC) stated that based on the precautionary principles, Europe had "the right to establish the level of protection—particularly of the environment, human, animal and plant health—that it deems appropriate." In further exposition, it argued: "The precautionary principle is not defined in the [1992 Treaty of the European Union], which prescribes it only once—to protect the environment. But *in practice*, its scope is much wider and specifically where preliminary objective scientific evaluation indicates that there are reasonable grounds for concern that the potentially dangerous effects on the *environment, human, animal, or plant health* may be inconsistent with the high level of protection chosen for the Community."[14] Equally significant, however, the EU has not provided a detailed definition of the principle in either the communication or any other official document.

In the WTO cases, though, the EU did employ one standard method of proof: a long list of international agreements, declarations, and national laws that allegedly are based on the precautionary principle (viz., 1987 Montreal Protocol [ozone], the 1992 Biodiversity Convention, the 1998 Chemicals Convention, the 1997 Kyoto Protocol, the 2000 Biosafety Protocol, and a number of others). What is interesting is that in most cases the precautionary principle was lodged in preambles and was thus largely a hortatory device and not a binding obligation.

In addition, the EU tackled the potentially limiting language of the SPS agreement. It posited that "scientific uncertainty as to cause and effect, magnitude, or severity is not an excuse to avoid employing precautionary measures, and that conventional science-based risk assessments required by SPS Article 5.1 are not enough, and must be bypassed, to prevent such hazards from materializing in the first place."[15]

In response, WTO panels and the Appellate Body have made two notable decisions in this area: the 1998 *EC – Hormones* decision and a panel decision in 2006, the *EC Biotech Products* decision. In 1998, the Appellate Body stated the following regarding the precautionary principle and CIL:

> The status of the precautionary principle in international law continues to be the subject of debate among academics, law practitioners, regulators and judges. The precautionary principle is regarded by some as having crystallized into a general principle of customary international environmental law. Whether it has been widely accepted by Members as a principle or general or customary international law appears less than clear. We consider, however, that it is unnecessary and probably imprudent, for the Appellate Body in this appeal to take a position on this important but abstract question. We note that the Panel itself did not make any definitive finding with regard

to the status of the precautionary principle in international law and that the precautionary principle, at least outside the field of international environmental law, still awaits authoritative formulation.[16]

The Appellate Body went on to deny the EU's contention that the precautionary principle allowed members to override the explicit language of the SPS agreement regarding scientific evidence and risk assessment. It noted, first, that "the principle has not been written into the SPS agreement as a ground for justifying SPS measures that are otherwise inconsistent with the obligations of Members set out in particular provisions of that Agreement." While member governments would take into account "perspectives of prudence and caution" when assessing whether "scientific evidence" warranted particular SPS measures, "the precautionary principle does not, by itself, and without a clear textual directive to that effect, relieve a [WTO] panel from the duty of applying the normal...principles of treaty interpretation in reading the provisions of the SPS agreement."[17] On this last point, what the Appellate Body was underscoring was that—even if the precautionary principle had some standing or relevance—normal rules of treaty interpretation would privilege the specific language of the SPS agreement over general principles of international law.

These issues were also discussed by a panel in a more recent case: *EC Biotech Products*, 2006. The panel first quoted portions of the Appellate Body's findings from 1998, noted above. It then went on to add:

> It appears to us from the Parties' arguments and other available material that the legal debate over whether the precautionary principle constitutes a recognized principle of general or customary international law is still ongoing. Notably, there has, to date, been no authoritative decision by an international court or tribunal which recognizes the precautionary principle as a principle of general or customary international law....Since the legal status of the precautionary principle remains unsettled, like the Appellate Body before us, we consider that prudence suggests that we not attempt to resolve this complex issue.[18]

Thus, up to this time, WTO panels and the Appellate Body have refused to take a position—under relevant WTO law—on the issues relating to the precautionary principle and CIL. But unfortunately, this sensible, "cautious" stance could change in the future. The 2006 panel quoted above based its decision in part on the fact that there has been "no authoritative decision by an international court or tribunal which recognizes the precautionary principle as a principle of general or customary international law."[19] But suppose in the future that the International Court of Justice did make such a finding? This would place the United States—and those who oppose the entire process by which customary law evolves in the contemporary setting—in a difficult position. The logic of the arguments made by scholars quoted earlier in this chapter—Rabkin, Goldsmith, and Trimble—would be to push the U.S. government to refuse to recognize such a ruling. Only through the U.S. political process—including a thorough public and congressional debate over the implications (and costs) of the precautionary principle—could such a dramatic change in policy be instituted.

The danger also exists that, even without a pronouncement by an international court, WTO panels and the Appellate Body could bow to shifting political winds and pressures. They have done so on key environmental questions in the past, most notably in the well-known *Shrimp-Turtle* decision in the late 1990s.[20] Oversimplifying somewhat, the case raised the question as to whether a WTO member (in this case the United States) could ban goods from another nation based on the "process" by which it was produced—or in this case on differences in environmental policies. An earlier GATT panel had ruled—correctly in the judgment here—that there was no legal precedent in GATT law upholding such a ban and that if GATT members wanted to permit such measures, "it would be preferable for them to do so not by interpreting Article XX [the exceptions clause cited above] but by amending or supplementing the provision of the General Agreement or waiving obligations thereunder—and not by judicial interpretation through the [dispute settlement system]."[21]

In the *Shrimp-Turtle* decision, however, the WTO Appellate Body adopted an "evolutionary interpretation" of WTO law (Article XX), stating that it "had to be read in light of contemporary concerns of the community of nations about protection and conservation of the environment." In support of what was a major amendment to GATT rules, the Appellate

Body merely referred to the preamble to the 1995 founding document that pledged to uphold the "conservation of natural resources."[22] The ruling produced an immediate backlash, particularly from developing countries, which saw it as opening the way for environmental coercion by large, developed economies, but WTO panels since then have cautiously built on such "evolutionary" interpretations to widen the gap between negotiated rules and judicial interpretation.

REACH, the Precautionary Principle, and the "Law's Migration"

One of the main topics in this volume has been on the EU's sweeping new regulations for chemicals: Registration, Evaluation, Authorisation and Restriction of Chemicals (REACH), which was approved in December 2006 and went into effect in June 2007. Ten years in the making, REACH regulations have generated huge controversies and a voluminous literature—technical, economic, and political. The following comments and analysis will be confined to issues raised previously in this chapter relating to the precautionary principle and the potential for international legal conflict.

Briefly, under REACH, all manufacturers and importers of chemicals into the EU are required to register any substance brought into the EU at a volume of one ton or more (estimates vary from thirty thousand to sixty-eight thousand chemicals, both new and existing). Registration is phased in, with substances counted as very harmful being processed first and less dangerous substances later (the process will be completed by 2018 under current plans). As part of the registration form, companies must supply a complete dossier, including comprehensive information about the chemical's properties and a toxicological analysis. For chemicals produced in quantities above ten metric tons, a more detailed safety report is required, which includes additional toxicological and exposure data and measures to reduce risk. A select group of products will be subject to an evaluation process, based on whether they will require further animal testing (an aim of REACH is to minimize animal testing) and whether they may present a high risk to human health or the environment. A third process—authorization—is reserved for a set of predetermined chemicals that are known to be highly toxic or dangerous: carcinogens, mutagens, and bioaccumulative or persistent organic pollutants. These will be authorized only after they pass a rigorous demonstration of risk control.[23] Producers must also present replacement plans or a research plan for alternatives.

In Article 1 of REACH, the EU declares that the "provisions are underpinned by the precautionary principle."[24] But as noted above, the precautionary principle has many definitions and applications. Within this wide scope for interpretation, there are three significant features of REACH that are important to note here. The first—and most significant—component of REACH is a complete reversal of the burden of proof: henceforth, rather than regulators having to demonstrate that a new or existing chemical is unsafe before taking action, it will be up to chemical manufacturers—a priori, before placing or continuing a substance on the market after registration—to demonstrate that the product is safe and does not "adversely affect human health or the environment."[25] Second, manufacturers will also be responsible for generating the resources and capital to produce the data backing up their claims of safety, and the lack of adequate data will be no defense against potential product bans. Cost has become a huge issue in the debate over REACH data analysis, as estimates vary from around $2 billion by the European Chemical Agency to $13.6 billion by a recent study funded by the European chemical industry.[26] As one commentator noted, however, the guiding principle is "no data, no market."[27] Third, EU bureaucrats have been granted enormous regulatory latitude to determine "how safe is safe" and options for market restrictions; and though there are vague references to "proportionality" and economic impact, effective cost/benefit analysis of the consequences of individual or collective decisions on chemicals is missing. There is, for instance, no attempt to reflect or mesh with the WTO's strictures at various junctures (SPS Agreement and Technical Barriers to Trade Agreement) to avoid "unnecessary obstacles to trade" or, as current U.S. policy demands, to adopt the "least burdensome" regulatory measures.

The international political history of REACH is fascinating and, ominously, quite possibly portentous. From the time the EC published a white paper in 2001 detailing its overall plan to push forward with REACH, a government-business coalition in the United States mounted a strong campaign to stop its passage and implementation. In the U.S. government, the State Department took the lead, supported by the Commerce Department, the Environmental Protection Agency, and the Office of the U.S. Trade Representative. From the private sector, the coalition consisted of a who's who of corporate associations, including, among others, the American Chemical Council, the American Plastics Council, the U.S. Council on International Business, and the National Association of Manufacturers. In 2002 and again in 2003, the then secretary of state Colin Powell sent urgent "action" cables to U.S. embassies in the EU and some thirty-odd other countries; and U.S. government officials remonstrated with relevant EU officials on numerous occasions from 2001 onward.

U.S. government and private sector executives offered wide-ranging criticisms of the proposed REACH regulations. They first pointed out that the U.S. government did not recognize the precautionary principle as a principle of international law, at one point describing it as a way to "provide cover for politically motivated bans and other severe restrictions."[28] Concomitantly, in various meetings and communications with European officials, the United States warned that REACH quite likely would violate the EU's WTO obligations, including strictures against discrimination and burdensome technical barriers to trade. In addition, they argued that implementation of REACH would cost businesses in the United States (and Europe) billions of dollars without compensatory benefits and that U.S. exporters would forfeit billions of dollars of exports. Extending the argument, they challenged Europe's determination to go forward without first conducting extensive cost/benefit analyses of the consequences of REACH, both within Europe and around the world. And Secretary Powell argued in talking points that the "complex regulatory approach" adopted in REACH ("the focus on tens of thousands of chemicals") was at odds with environmentally "sound management...that better balances risk and economic considerations."[29]

By and large, both the campaign and the arguments that underpinned it failed to move European officials. Though there were some accommodating changes as the legislative and administrative process progressed, to a great degree REACH emerged much as it was originally conceived. Furthermore, after prodding the U.S. government continuously and strenuously from 2001 through 2007, U.S. business groups folded their tents and in effect admitted defeat. Although business organizations still publicly complain about aspects of REACH, in off-the-record interviews they concede that at this point their main efforts are to adapt to REACH's highly complex substantive and procedural requirements. All in all, it is an extraordinary turnaround. Similarly, even before the advent of the Obama administration, Bush administration officials had ceased their heavy criticisms of REACH; and there are no longer any threats to institute WTO actions alleging violations of Europe's trade obligations. And the Obama administration, staffed by many committed environmentalists and former NGOs that had applauded REACH, is not likely to revive the earlier U.S. anti-REACH campaign.

So what are the lessons and consequences—at least to date—from the REACH experience? First, despite the misgivings and opposition of the United States (and other nations, particularly from the developing world), a more stringent and intrusive version of the precautionary principle is now likely to dominate the regulatory universe for chemicals. The successful EU decision (and export of that decision) to reverse the burden of proof as a standard for chemical regulation alone is a huge win for a more "advanced" interpretation of the precautionary principle. It remains to be seen if this momentous change will be adopted for other regulatory actions.

Second, and of equal importance, is the process by which REACH unfolded, first as a domestic choice of the EU, but now increasingly as a force for change internationally. What seems to be occurring is a process that is standing the usual interpretation of "competition-based regulation" on its head. Rather than a competition leading to more "market-friendly" solutions, the extension of the highly intrusive and costly REACH regulations internationally will likely set off a "race to the top," by which is meant a competition for greater government intervention in the name of a more extreme version of the precautionary principle. Whatever the consequences, it must be said that, at least until now, the EU has triumphed through sheer force of political will—or, more accurately, bureaucratic will.

Finally, the rationale for REACH was based directly on the EU's interpretation of the precautionary principle and thus constitutes state action, not the more ephemeral writings and opinions of academics and NGOs. It may well advance the day when an international tribunal announces that the precautionary principle has reached the status of the "law of custom," a result that would have large repercussions and trigger huge international legal conflicts.

Notes

1. "Wingspread Statement on the Precautionary Principle," Wingspread Conference on the Precautionary Principle, Johnson Foundation, Racine, Wisconsin, http://www.sehn.org/wing.html.

2. United Nations, "2000 Cartagena Protocol on Biosafety" (addendum to UN Convention on Biological Diversity), 2000, http://www.cbd.int/doc/legal/cartagena-protocol-en.pdf.

3. United Nations, "Rio Declaration on Environment and Development," adopted at UN Conference on Environment and Development, 1992, http://www.unep.org/Documents.Multilingual/Default.asp?DocumentID=78&ArticleID=1163 (emphasis added).

4. Robert W. Hahn and Cass R. Sunstein, "The Precautionary Principle as a Basis for Decision Making," *Economists' Voice* (2005): 1–2, http://www.bepress.com/ev/vol2/iss2/art8/; for a recent defense of the use of the precautionary principle in decision making, see Elampara Deloso, "The Precautionary Principle: Relevance in International Law and Climate Change," Lund University Master's Programme in International Environmental Science, Lund University, Sweden, 2005, http://www.lumes.lu.se/database/alumni/04.05/theses/rabbi_deloso.pdf.

5. World Trade Organization, "European Communities: Measures Affecting the Approval and Marketing of Biotech Products" (report of the panel), WT/DS291/R, WT/DS292/R, and WT/DS293/R, paragraph 337 (hereinafter *EC Biotech Products*), 2006, http://www.wto.org/english/tratop_e/dispu_e/cases_e/ds293_e.htm.

6. For the EU argument, see World Trade Organization, "EC Measures concerning Meat and Meat Products," WT/DS26/R and WT/DS48, 1998, paragraphs 120–122, http://www.wto.org/english/tratop_E/dispu_e/cases_e/ds26_e.htm; see also the more complete defense of EU's invocation of the precautionary principle in Commission of the European Communities, "Communication from the Commission on the Precautionary Principle," Brussels, 2000 (hereinafter "EC Communication"), http://ec.europa.eu/dgs/health_consumer/library/pub/pub07_en.pdf.

7. Jeremy Rabkin, *Why Sovereignty Matters* (Washington, DC: AEI Press, 1996), 32–33. These issues, and the tie-in to the WTO, are also discussed in Claude E. Barfield, *Free Trade, Sovereignty, Democracy: The Future of the World Trade Organization* (Washington, DC: AEI Press, 2001), 58–69.

8. Rabkin, *Why Sovereignty Matters*, 55; for a critique of the process by which legal theorists attempt to establish the legitimacy of customary international law by an author sympathetic to environmental causes, see Daniel Bodansky, "Customary (and Not So Customary) International Environmental Law," *Indiana Journal of Global Legal Studies* 3 (1995): 105–19, http://www.heinonline.org/HOL/Page? handle=hein.journals/ijgls3&id=111&size=2&collection=journals&set_as_ cursor=0.

9. Curtis A. Bradley and Jack L. Goldsmith, "Customary International Law as Federal Common Law: A Critique of the Modern Position," *Harvard Law Review* 110 (1997): 47–48 (footnotes omitted), http://www.jstor.org/pss/1342230.

10. Ibid.

11. Philip R. Trimble, "A Revisionist View of Customary International Law," *UCLA Law Review* 33 (1986): 718, 721. For a view challenging the assertion that CIL threatens U.S. democratic institutions, see Joel Richard Paul, "Is Global Governance Safe for Democracy?" *Chicago Journal of International Law* 1 (2000): 263–71, http://heinonline.org/HOL/Page?collection=journals&handle=hein. journals/cjil1&id=271.

12. Implementing the precautionary principle also raises issues for the WTO Technical Barriers to Trade Agreement, but for reasons of space, these matters will not be analyzed here.

13. For a more detailed analysis of WTO health regulations, biotech foods, and WTO agreements, see Nick Covelli and Viktor Hohots, "The Health Regulation of Biotech Foods under the WTO Agreements," *Journal of International Economic Law* 6 (2003): 773–95, http://jiel.oxfordjournals.org/cgi/reprint/6/4/773; and Reinhard Quick and Andreas Bluthner, "Has the Appellate Body Erred? An Appraisal and Criticism of the Ruling in the WTO *Hormones Case*," *Journal of International Economic Law* 2 (1999): 603–39, http://jiel.oxfordjournals.org/cgi/reprint/2/4/603.

14. EC Communication, 1.

15. Lawrence A. Kogan, "WTO Ruling on Biotech Food Addresses the 'Precautionary Principle,'" *Legal Backgrounder*, Washington Legal Foundation, December 8, 2006, 2, http://www.itssd.org/Publications/wto-biotech-foods-dec0806.pdf.

16. World Trade Organization, "EC Measures concerning EC Meat and Meat Products," paragraph 124.

17. Ibid.

18. *EC Biotech Products*, paragraph 7.89.

19. Ibid.

20. World Trade Organization, "United States—Import Prohibition of Certain Shrimp and Shrimp Products," Appellate Body, WT/DS58/AB/R, 1998, http://www. wto.org/english/tratop_E/dispu_e/cases_e/ds58_e.htm.

21. World Trade Organization, "United States—Restrictions on Imports of Tuna," Report of the Panel, Circulated but not Adopted, September 1991, http://www. temple.edu/lawschool/drwiltext/docs/Tuna%20Dolphin%202.pdf.

22. Barfield, *Free Trade, Sovereignty, Democracy*, 46–48.

23. Obviously, this brief description of REACH omits many details: for greater depth of description, see Doaa Abdel Motaal, "Reaching REACH: The Challenge for Chemicals Entering International Trade," *Journal of International Economic Law* 12 (2009): 543–662, http://jiel.oxfordjournals.org/cgi/content/full/jgp027. For analyses highly sympathetic to REACH, see John Applegate, "Synthesizing TASCA and REACH: Practical Principles for Chemical Regulation Reform," *Ecology Law Quarterly* 35 (2009): 35, 721ff., http://heinonline.org/HOL/Page?collection=journals&handle=hein.journals/eclawq35&id=729; and Joanne Scott, "From Brussels with Love: The Transatlantic Travels of European Law and the Chemistry of Regulatory Attraction," *American Journal of Comparative Law* 52 (2009): 897–942, http://heinonline.org/HOL/Page?collection=journals&handle=hein.journals/amcomp57&id=907. For an unremitting, and prolific, critic of REACH, see the studies of Lawrence A. Kogan, especially Kogan, "WTO Ruling," and Lawrence A. Kogan, "Exporting Precaution: How Europe's Risk-Free Regulatory Agenda Threatens American Free Enterprise," Washington Legal Foundation, Washington, DC, 2005, http://www.wlf.org/upload/110405MONOKogan.pdf.

24. European Commission, "Regulation 1907/2006 (Concerning the Registration, Evaluation, Authorisation and Restriction of Chemicals (REACH), Establishing a European Chemicals Agency," 2507 O.J. (L136), 1, http://eur-lex.europa.eu/LexUriServ/LexUriServ.do?uri=oj:l:2006:396:0001:0849:en:pdf.

25. Applegate, "Synthesizing TASCA," 25.

26. Natasha Gilbert, "Chemical-Safety Costs Uncertain," *Nature*, August 27, 2009, http://www.nature.com /news/2009/090826/pdf/4601065a.pdf.

27. Applegate, "Synthesizing TASCA," 24. An ancillary concern stems from the strong pressures ("incentives") in REACH for manufacturers to share information with other manufacturers in order to reduce data costs and to share also with "the public"—that is, NGOs. Despite assurances of confidentiality for proprietary information, many chemical manufacturers remain skeptical of the protection of vital information.

28. Much of this section is taken from a very hostile, but credible, account by an antiglobal NGO: Joseph DiGangi, "REACH and the Long Arm of the Chemical Industry," *Multinational Monitor*, September 1, 2004, 4, http://www.multinationa monitor.org/mm2004/092004/digangi.html. DiGangi had obtained government documents and memos through the Freedom of Information Act and from anonymous sources.

29. Ibid., 6.

7

Feeding a Hungry World: Opportunity and Obligation for U.S. Agriculture

Douglas Nelson and Alexander Rinkus

Crop protection products have long played a significant role in agriculture. Since humanity evolved from nomadic hunting and gathering to a sedentary agrarian people, we have struggled to provide for ourselves while battling the pests of nature that compete with us for the same food. The fossil record demonstrates that insects from 390 million years ago fed on early land plants, while humans have cultivated those same plants for only 10,000 years. Insects have obviously had a long head start on capturing the nutrients of these plants for themselves. Without a consistent way to feed ourselves, empires have fallen and wars have been waged in the battle to maintain an adequate food supply. It was only two centuries ago that new methods for pest control fueled population growth and spurred an intellectual revolution that has not ceased.

The new methods began in France in the mid nineteenth century. During the 1850s a breakout of powdery mildew devastated the grape-growing French countryside. An easy-to-spot disease, powdery mildew appears as a white powderlike substance on plant leaves. Beginning as small spots, the infection grows and eventually moves up the stem of the infected host. With the substance blocking the sun, plant cells cannot photosynthesize, leading to reduced vine growth, yield, and grape quality. The infection permits the interior of the fruit to grow while the epidermal skin does not. Eventually the inner grape pulp will burst through the outer skin. Grapes that do survive are reported as having an "off taste" and deemed unacceptable for wine production. Prior to infection, annual wine production in France reached approximately one billion gallons. By the mid-1800s, famers were struggling to produce barely two hundred million gallons. In 1854 alone, 80 percent of French grape yields were lost.[1] Wine prices doubled, and the government immediately abolished all import taxes on spirits in order to satisfy the French appetite for alcohol and keep an unhappy populace in check. Then, scientists discovered that ground sulfur, when properly applied to a plant, would kill the fungus.[2] When sulfur is applied, it mixes with hydrogen produced by the powdery mildew to create hydrogen sulfide, a gas toxic to the powdery mildew. News of this discovery spread immediately throughout France, and by 1858 wine production had returned to its previous levels. This revolutionary use of sulfur was the first major crop protection product. Prior to this, losing between 20 percent and 100 percent of crop yields in any given year was a fact of life for a farmer, an unavoidable consequence of battling pests.

After two decades of production stability, a new iteration of mildew, downy mildew, appeared within French grape orchards. This mildew left plant leaves stricken with water-soaked black spots that grew until they killed the plant. Grape production once again plummeted, prices skyrocketed, and the volatile French populace began to grumble. Not until 1878 was an effective control found for this disease, and it was discovered almost by accident. French botanist Alexis Millardet witnessed a farmer spraying his plants with a blue mixture of lime and copper sulfate in order to discourage pilferers. When visiting the orchard later, the scientist observed that the plants that had been sprayed were healthy and uninfected while those that were not sprayed were stricken with disease. He discovered that the copper ions of the mixture were toxic to the fungus and that the lime acted as a protectant to the grapes, reducing the damage from the copper sulfate.[3] This mixture was named Bordeaux mixture after the region, and crop production was eternally changed.

Bordeaux mixture, unlike sulfur, controlled downy mildew infections across a wide range of crops. This was especially important in food staple crops. Only a few decades earlier, the Great Famine of Ireland had been caused by the worst outbreak of potato blight ever seen. The population starved while fields went fallow. Bordeaux mixture had the ability to control blight in potatoes. By the early 1900s Bordeaux mixture was used extensively on potatoes throughout North America and Europe. In World War I, when a major blight epidemic on potatoes went untreated, German potatoes rotted in the fields. The resulting scarcity led to the deaths of seven hundred thousand German civilians from starvation and created severe demoralization in the German army.[4]

Witnessing the effectiveness of Bordeaux mixture, chemists of the early twentieth century experimented with a wide range of products to see if they could control other diseases, insects, and weeds that pervaded farmers' fields. They found that arsenic, sulfur, and Bordeaux were the three major chemicals able to offer effective controls of certain pests. In the 1930s, U.S. chemists worked to design new compounds. These synthetic compounds were produced specifically for pest control. The first synthetic chemicals, nabam, thiram, and zineb, were patented in the late 1930s, and their fungicidal properties were confirmed in 1941 by the Connecticut Agricultural Research Station.[5] These research stations were the first foray by the government into the development of synthetic crop protection chemicals. The wartime government of the 1940s was particularly eager to maintain steady and abundant food supply, so money poured into these stations to improve pest control methods and reduce preventable crop losses. At the Connecticut station alone, more than six thousand compounds were tested for possible usefulness.[6] The war effort spurred the government and the crop protection industry to work in concert for decades to come.

With industry and government working in tandem, synthetic chemical compounds for crop protection were produced at an unprecedented pace. As figure 7-1 indicates, the introduction of effective synthetic pesticides at mid-century decreased the need for farm labor. In the United States two-thirds of the population in the nineteenth century were required to be farmers in order to feed the country.[7] When farms could control pests and boost yields to their peak, however, it allowed agriculture to support an emerging industrial economy. From 1920 to 1980, farm labor declined by more than 70 percent. Where farmers previously hired labor to pull weeds and remove insects during high infection seasons, they now utilized labor-saving products to protect against these infections. Children who previously left school to help pull weeds during peak weed season were now able to focus on their studies. Crop protection products were the avenue by which not just the United States but also the global economy could reach its full potential. The CropLife Foundation estimates that if farmers were to return to using labor instead of crop protection products to pull weeds, U.S. agriculture would need approximately seventy-two million (approximately 23 percent of total U.S .population) additional farm laborers to maintain current yields.[8]

FIGURE 7-1

U.S. FARM LABOR LEVELS RELATIVE TO 1950

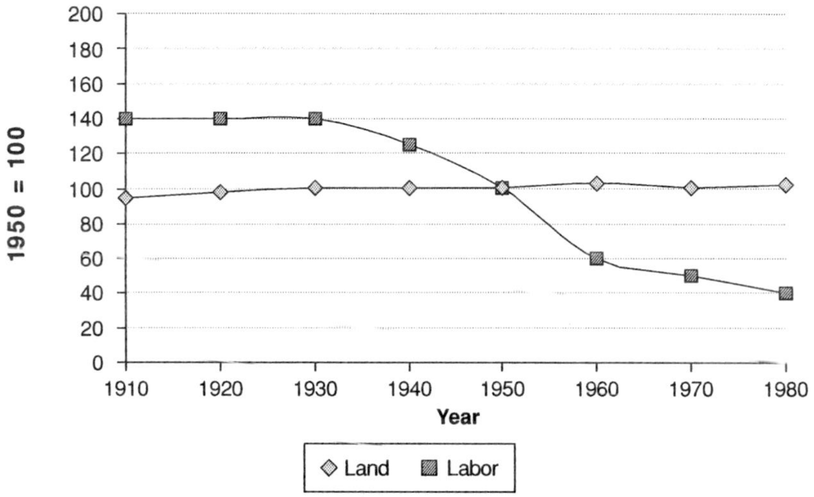

SOURCES: Data 1910–1950 from Ralph A. Loomis and Glen T. Barton, "Productivity of Agriculture: United States, 1870–1958," U.S. Department of Agriculture, 1961. Data 1950–1980 from USDA-ERS.

By using these technologies in a targeted and effective manner, we have been able to feed a growing population with fewer workers on the same amount of land. The U.S. population has quadrupled during the past century, but arable land has remained the same.[9] In 1890 there were 27.5 acres per farm worker in the United States. In 1990, each farm worker represented 740 acres.[10] This means we have not just a more effective industry but also one that provides for the rest of the population efficiently and economically. At the turn of the nineteenth century, U.S. consumers were spending approximately half of their income on food-stuffs.[11] By the 1950s the share of food as a slice of annual income was down to 29.7 percent, and by 2002 it had fallen to 13.1 percent.[12] Today the average American spends only $42.50 on food per week.[13] This means that a mere $2,210 can assure food security for the average American for the entire year. These gains translate to a more streamlined and effective U.S. agriculture economy, with crop protection products being the catalyst. As figures 7-2, 7-3, and 7-4 demonstrate, farmers in the United States have been able to boost yields of major crops to record levels while, as noted earlier, utilizing less labor than ever. These advancements began in 1950, when synthetic crop protection products were introduced, providing consistent protection against pests for all major crops. As table 7-1 demonstrates, without crop protection products, major U.S. crops would be faced with staggering yield losses, and the American consumer could be faced with skyrocketing prices. Therefore, the key component in reducing the cost of food is high and consistent yields, which crop protection products ensure. These products enable just 2 percent of our population to provide for the other 98 percent. Understanding this history is key to participating in the robust and necessary debate surrounding the use of crop protection products and the important benefits farmers and consumers realize through their use.

FIGURE 7-2
U.S. CORN YIELDS, 1880–1970

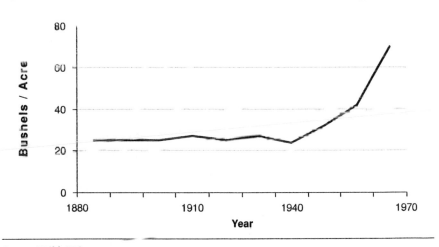

SOURCE: USDA-ERS.

TABLE 7-1
U.S. CROP LOSSES WITHOUT INSECTICIDES

Crop	% Reduction	Billion Pounds
Apples	−93	9.2
Oranges	−61	9.0
Peaches	−54	1.0
Peanuts	−50	1.9
Potatoes	−29	11.9
Tomatoes	−52	13.4

SOURCE: Leonard Gianessi, "Benefits of Insecticides in U.S. Crop Production," CropLife Foundation, 2008.

For example, the three most valuable crops right now, according to the USDA, are corn, wheat, and soybeans. They are valued at $47.4 billion, $16.6 billion, and $27.4 billion, respectively, or approximately 68 percent of the United States' $134 billion crop production industry.[14] If yields of these crops were reduced, the repercussion would impact not just U.S. agriculture but also the U.S. role in the global economy. Using USDA data, the CropLife Foundation has estimated that U.S. corn yields would fall 20 percent without the use of herbicides, wheat production would decline by 19 percent without the use of fungicides, and soybean production would plummet 26 percent without the use of insecticides.[15] Less domestic crop production would inevitably result in more imports from other nations. In fact, Brazil, France, and Japan, three prominent trade rivals, are increasing their use of crop protection technologies and increasing agricultural exports. If we were to reduce the use of domestic crop protection products, our famers would not be able to compete in the global agriculture market, potentially forcing many U.S. farmers out of business and risking our domestic ability to feed ourselves in a sustainable manner.

With crop protection products as the basis of an effective and efficient American agricultural system, we can use new technological advances to enhance our productivity. Advanced fertilizers being introduced to the market each year enable farmers to boost their yields by producing larger

FIGURE 7-3
U.S. RICE YIELDS, 1899–1989

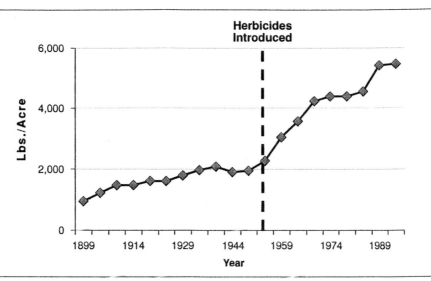

SOURCE: USDA-ERS.

and more productive crops. However, fertilizers are incredibly dependent on crop protection products to realize their full value. The key to fertilizer use is proper weed control. If a farmer fertilizes a crop without controlling weeds, he is not only fertilizing his plants but also inadvertently fertilizing the weeds. This situation could result in larger, more robust weeds that would rob the farmer's crops of precious nutrients needed to reach their full potential. Without herbicide technology to eliminate weeds, fertilizers would be assisting the invasive pests that damage the crop.

Along with advanced fertilizer technology, twenty-first-century agriculture has seen the introduction of modern seed innovations that allow farmers to grow crops with specialty traits genetically introduced into the seed itself. In the case of soybeans and corn, these traits have been devised to allow the use of more targeted crop protection products. These products are not only more effective and environmentally friendly but also save the farmer input costs and keep his land more productive for a longer period of time. Since their inception, biotech crops have been grown on a larger segment of U.S. agriculture land every year. Farmers recognize the inherent benefits in these products as smart business and are growing higher quality crops for less money. The National Center for Food and Agricultural Policy estimated in a comprehensive study that biotech crops in 2005 alone boosted U.S. agricultural production by 8.34 billion pounds, reduced production costs by $1.4 billion, and boosted profits by $2 billion.[16] Researchers have estimated that worldwide these crops are increasing farmer income by $4.8–$6.5 billion and providing a higher quality product due to less insect, weed, and fungus damage.[17] We have also been able to replace past fuel-intensive agronomic practices with precision agricultural techniques, such as no-till farming, which enhances sustainability and reduces the environmental footprint. Studies show that, since 1996, biotech crops have saved farmers 441 million gallons of fuel through reduced fuel operations, which eliminates nearly 10.2 million pounds of carbon dioxide emissions or the equivalent of removing four million cars from the road.[18] The future holds only further potential for these crops and their benefits. Crops that are drought resistant will be able to assist farmers in the developing world as they struggle in lands that are ill suited for farming. Crops that produce healthier oils can reduce obesity and positively

FIGURE 7-4
U.S. WHEAT PRODUCTION, 1900–2009

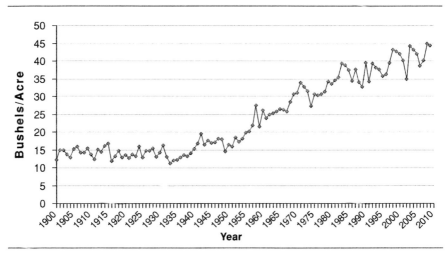

SOURCE: USDA-ERS.

affect other health-related issues. The possibilities in our lifetime and beyond are nearly endless.

As closely linked as agriculture is to our lives, we need to ensure that all farm inputs are safe and being used properly. The U.S. government has created a rigorous testing process that any modern agriculture technology must successfully complete before reaching the U.S. consumer. From discovery to submission to registration by the Environmental Protection Agency, a company will spend approximately ten years and nearly $260 million to ensure the safety of the product when used properly.[19] This process not just reduces risk but negates virtually any risk. Under the Federal Insecticide, Fungicide, and Rodenticide Act, the U.S. government has declared that for a product to reach the hands of a U.S. farmer and be applied to the food any American could eat, it must be demonstrated that it "perform[s] its intended function without unreasonable adverse effects on the environment" and that "there is a reasonable certainty that no harm will result from aggregate exposure to the pesticide chemical residue."[20] With other ubiquitous products, such as cars, some harm is likely and unavoidable; the goal is to reduce harm as much as possible. Crop protection products are held to a standard like no other. The expectation is that any harm is to be virtually eliminated. With this goal in mind, the industry, after fulfilling EPA requirements, makes products that include detailed directions on where the product can be applied, the necessary application and safety equipment, relevant restrictions for product use, where and how to store the product, and how to rinse and dispose of a container.

In this chapter we have noted the important role that crop protection products play in today's society. In part because of these products, food security has moved from a constant struggle to a right and expectation in the developed world. We should also note, however, that many people in the developing world do not know where their next meal will come from. The United Nations Food and Agriculture Organization estimates that one billion people were undernourished in 2009. The organization also identifies two parallel tracks to ending this crisis. The first track is solving the short-term deficiencies by providing developing countries with direct access to food through food aid, cash transfers, and safety nets. The second track is the long-term solution that will allow countries to independently produce enough for themselves by strengthening productivity and income through better infrastructure, science, and technology.[21] By bringing new plant sciences and technologies to the people of the developing world, we can set them on the path the developed world has tread for almost two centuries. By giving the people of developing world the opportunity to leave the farm to receive a formal education and develop skills beyond manual labor, a second information revolution could parallel a second green revolution. By 2050, the UN estimates that the world population will be as high as nine billion people.[22] If we can adequately feed all nine billion and give them the opportunity to fulfill their intellectual promise, there is truly no predicting where humanity can go in the next century. Plant science and technology is the vehicle that can take us there.

Notes

1. Frederic T. Bioletti, "Oidium or Powdery Mildew of the Vine," *Bulletin No. 186*, University of California Agricultural Experiment Station (February 1907).

2. D. M. Spencer, ed., *The Powdery Mildews* (New York: Academic Press, 1978).

3. Gail L. Schumann, *Plant Diseases: Their Biology and Social Impact* (St. Paul, MN: APS Press, 1991).

4. George Wong, "The Origin of Plant Pathology and the Potato Famine, and Other Stories of Plant Diseases," University of Hawaii, 2003, http://www.botany. hawaii.edu/faculty/wong/BOT135/LECT06.htm; G. L. Carefoot and E. R. Sprott, *Famine on the Wind: Man's Battle against Plant Disease* (Chicago: Rand McNally, 1967).

5. Gordon A. Brandes, "The History and Development of the Ethylene Bisdithiocarbamate Fungicides," *American Potato Journal* 30 (1953): 137.

6. U.S. Department of Agriculture, "Experiment Station Progress in Insect and Plant Disease Control," 1945, Agricultural Research Administration, OES-R1, 1946.

7. USDA Agriculture in the Classroom, "A History of Agriculture: 1850," http://www.agclassroom.org/gan/timeline/farmers_land.htm.

8. Leonard Gianessi and Sujatha Sankula, "Benefits of Herbicides in U.S. Crop Production," CropLife Foundation, 2005, 41, http://www.croplifefoundation.org/ Documents/Pesticide%20Benefits/Herbicides/HerbBeniFullText.pdf.

9. U.S. Census Bureau, "Historical National Population Estimates: July 1, 1990 to July 1, 1999," http://www.census.gov/popest/archives/1990s/pop clockest.txt; USDA-ERS, "Major Uses of Land in the United States, 2002," http://www. ers.usda.gov/publications/EIB14/.

10. U.S. Environmental Protection Agency, "Demographics," http://www.epa. gov/oecaagct/ag101/demographics.html.

11. U.S. Bureau of Labor Statistics, "100 Years of Consumer Spending: 1901," http://www.bls.gov/opub/uscs/1901.pdf.

12. U.S. Bureau of Labor Statistics, "100 Years of Consumer Spending: 1950," http://www.bls.gov/opub/uscs/1950.pdf; ibid., "100 Years of Consumer Spending: 2002–03," http://www.bls.gov/opub/uscs/2002-03.pdf.

13. USDA-ERS, "Household Food Security in the United States, 2008," http://www.ers.usda.gov/Publications/ERR83/ERR83c.pdf.

14. USDA-NASS, "Crop Statistics," http://www.nass.usda.gov/Statistics_by_Subject/index.asp#.

15. Leonard Gianessi and Sujatha Sankula, "The Value of Herbicides in U.S. Crop Production: 2005 Update," CropLife Foundation, 2005, http://www.crop lifefoundation.org/cpri/_benefits_herbicides.htm; Leonard Gianessi, "Benefits of Fungicides in U.S. Crop Production," CropLife Foundation, 2005, http://www.croplifefoundation.org/cpri_benefits_fungicides.htm; Leonard Gianessi, "Benefits of Insecticides in U.S. Crop Production," CropLife Foundation, 2008, http://www.croplifefoundation.org/cpri_benefits_insecticides.htm.

16. Sujatha Sankula, "Quantification of the Impacts on U.S. Agriculture of Biotechnology-Derived Crops Planted in 2005," National Center for Food and Agricultural Policy, http://www.ncfap.org/documents/2005biotechExec Summary.pdf.

17. C. Ford Runge and Barry Ryan, "The Global Diffusion of Plant Biotechnology: International Adoption and Research in 2004," http://www.agrobio.org/documents/Biblioteca/The%20Global%20Diffusion%20of%20Plant%20 Biotechnology.pdf.

18. Graham Brookes, "Global Impact of Biotech Crops: Socio-Economic and Environmental Effects in the First Ten Years of Commercial Use," http://www.pgeconomics.co.uk/Global_impact_of_biotech_crops.htmPG Economics.

19. Phillips McDougall, "The Cost of New Agrochemical Product Discovery, Development and Registration and Research and Development Predictions for the Future," January 2010, http://www.croplifeamerica.org/sites/default/files/node_images/PM%20R%26D%20Study_2%2025%2010.pdf.

20. U.S. Environmental Protection Agency, "Federal Insecticide, Fungicide, and Rodenticide Act (FIFRA)," http://www.epa.gov/agriculture/lfra.html.

21. United Nations Food and Agriculture Organization, "Food Insecurity in the World: 2009," ftp://ftp.fao.org/docrep/fao/012/i0876e/i0876e.pdf.

22. United Nations, "World Population Will Increase by 2.5 Billion by 2050," press release, March 13, 2007, http://www.un.org/News/Press/docs//2007/pop952.doc.htm.

Index

143

About the Authors

Jonathan H. Adler is a professor of law and director of the Center for Business Law and Regulation at the Case Western Reserve University School of Law, where he teaches courses in environmental, regulatory, and constitutional law. Prior to joining the Case faculty, Mr. Adler clerked for the Honorable David B. Sentelle on the U.S. Court of Appeals for the District of Columbia Circuit. He also worked as the director of environmental studies for the Competitive Enterprise Institute. Mr. Adler's writing focuses primarily on environmental and regulatory policy issues. He is the author or editor of four books, including *The Costs of Kyoto: Climate Change Policy and Its Implications* (Competitive Enterprise Institute, 1997) and *Environmentalism at the Crossroads* (Capital Research Center, 1995), and several book chapters. His work has appeared in publications ranging from the *Harvard Environmental Law Review* and the *Supreme Court Economic Review* to the *Wall Street Journal* and the *Washington Post*. In 2004, Mr. Adler received the Paul M. Bator Award, given annually by the Federalist Society for Law and Policy Studies to an academic under forty for excellence in teaching, scholarship, and commitment to students. In 2007, the Case Western Reserve University Law Alumni Association awarded Mr. Adler its annual Distinguished Teacher Award.

Claude Barfield is a resident scholar at the American Enterprise Institute. He is the author or editor of a number of books on trade and science policy, including *Biotechnology and the Patent System: Balancing Innovation and Property Rights* (AEI Press, 2007), *High-Tech Protectionism: The Irrationality of Antidumping Laws* (AEI Press, 2003), and *Free Trade, Sovereignty, Democracy: The Future of the World Trade Organization* (AEI Press, 2001). Before joining AEI, Mr. Barfield served in the Gerald R. Ford administration on the staff of the Senate Governmental Affairs Committee and as a co-staff director of the President's Commission for a National Agenda for the Eighties.

Jon Entine is a visiting fellow at the American Enterprise Institute. A former Emmy-winning producer for NBC News and ABC News, he researches and writes about corporate responsibility, science, and advocacy groups (NGOs). His books include *No Crime but Prejudice: Fischer Homes, the Immigration Fiasco, and Extra-Judicial Prosecution* (TFG Books, 2009), about prosecutorial excesses; *Abraham's Children: Race, Identity, and the DNA of the Chosen People* (Grand Central Publishing, 2007), which focuses on the genetics of race; *Let Them Eat Precaution: How Politics Is Undermining the Genetic Revolution in Agriculture* (AEI Press, 2006); and the best-selling *Taboo: Why Black Athletes Dominate Sports and Why We're Afraid to Talk about It* (PublicAffairs, 2001), based on an award-winning NBC News documentary. Mr. Entine is also a columnist for *Ethical Corporation* magazine and founder of a sustainability consultancy, ESG MediaMetrics.

Euros Jones has worked for the European Crop Protection Association (ECPA) since May 2001 and has been director of Regulatory Affairs since January 2006. He previously worked for the National Farmers' Union as deputy director of the Brussels office and for the European Council of Young Farmers as secretary general. In his current post, Mr. Jones's responsibilities include supporting ECPA's advocacy on regulatory issues dealing with the marketing and use of plant protection products and their residues in food.

Douglas Nelson is executive vice president, general counsel, and secretary of CropLife America, the largest U.S. trade organization representing developers, manufacturers, formulators, and distributors of agricultural crop protection products. He also sits on the board of directors of CropLife Foundation, a 501(c)(3) educational and research foundation promoting sustainable agriculture and the environmentally safe use of crop protection products and bio-engineered agriculture. Mr. Nelson is also an appointed member of the United States Industry Trade Advisory Committee on Intellectual Property Rights. Prior to working at CropLife America, Mr. Nelson was assistant general counsel and assistant secretary of Unilever United States, Inc., in New York City; he also served as Acquisitions and Divestitures counsel at Union Carbide Corporation in Danbury, Connecticut, and as an associate lawyer in the New York law firms of Paul, Weiss, Rifkind, Wharton and Garrison, and Coudert Brothers. Mr. Nelson is an adjunct lecturer at the Johns Hopkins University, teaching graduate-level courses on corporations, business law, and globalization, and has taught at American University's Washington School of Law, Columbia University, North Carolina State University, Brooklyn College, and the New School for Social Research.

Alexander Rinkus is a researcher at CropLife Foundation, a 501(c)(3) educational and research foundation promoting sustainable agriculture and the environmentally safe use of crop protection products and bio-engineered agriculture. Mr. Rinkus also consults for CropLife International, a global federation representing the plant science industry. Prior to joining CropLife Foundation, he worked with the National Academy of Public Administration and the National Pork Producers Council.

Richard Tren is a founder and the director of the health policy and advocacy group Africa Fighting Malaria (AFM), which has offices in South Africa and the United States. AFM is one of the few malaria advocacy groups that promotes the increased use of indoor spraying of insecticides for malaria control and has advocated for more random testing of pharmaceuticals in the developing world. Mr. Tren has researched and written widely on health and development, with a particular focus on malaria and other communicable diseases. His most recent book is *The Excellent Powder: DDT's Political and Scientific History* (Dog Ear Publishing, 2010). Mr. Tren is a council member of the Free Market Foundation of Southern Africa and was the 2009 recipient of the Julian Simon Award.

Mark Whalon directs the Pesticide Alternatives Laboratory at Michigan State University, where he has been a professor of entomology since 1979. His current research emphases include applied fruit integrated pest management (IPM), resistance pest management, biopesticide development and adoption, and organic pest management. Mr. Whalon is also involved in national and international policy on IPM, ecological impacts of pesticides, pesticide resistance management, and various conventional and organic materials registration and certification. He currently serves on three federal advisory committees and serves as the secretary to the Organic Materials Review Institute Advisory Board.

Jeanette Wilson is an entomological tree fruit systems technician and laboratory aide in the Pesticide Alternatives Laboratory at Michigan State University.